Melinda & Robert
Schoutens

FRESH AIR KIDS
SWITZERLAND

FRESH AIR KIDS SWITZERLAND

Hikes to Huts:
Adventures for the Kid Inside Us All

Melinda & Robert
Schoutens

HELVETIQ

To our two miraculous children,
Thank you for being our most valued treasures, our clearest crystals and our shiniest stones. May you understand that mountains climbed are a physical metaphor that serve to teach us that everything of value in this life requires tenacity and heart. Carry those lessons close to you and allow them to guide all that you do. Remember to believe in yourselves and be willing to venture into the unknown. For us, as your parents, those unknowns have created the greatest joy of our lives, and that includes the two of you. Continue to shine and share your gifts with the world!

To Anne,
I am forever grateful to you for gracefully revealing how to cultivate a life well lived; a life abundant with love and acceptance and a dash of crazy. You elevated my life with the lessons you shared, the journeys we endured and the conversations that left me a better person. I will always remember the inspiration you sprinkled along all of the paths we crossed together. Until we meet again.

Melinda

"

You have a whole life in the outdoors, you realize you have a sense of responsibility to protect the wild places.

"

YVON CHOUINARD,
ENVIRONMENTALIST, OUTDOORSMAN,
FOUNDER OF PATAGONIA

To our readers,
Because of you, we are committed to making a donation to a non-profit organization that strives to help preserve and protect the environment. Our collective footprints are weighing heavily on the Earth. As we continue to step into the natural world, we must remember to do so with deep regard and respect. May we make conscious decisions that create a hopeful future for our children. This land, and our world, are worth protecting.

Contents

Map of Hikes

Out-and-back ⟲   Point-to-point ⬌   Loop ◯   Tour ⬌

CHAPTER I

The Joy of the Mountains

"

Going to the mountains is going home.

"

JOHN MUIR
NATURALIST AND AUTHOR

Our love for the mountains has yet to wane. We find ourselves growing increasingly restless whenever we are away from the Alps for too long. Our children experience that same longing, as they delight in the freedom that only nature can provide. Their sense of discovery is tenacious and their inquisitive souls long to make sense of the world around them. They excite in the possibility of locating frogs and spotting salamanders on the trails. Their smiles are delightful to witness as butterflies come into view and land on them. They are mesmerized by nature's ability to provide all they need for wild entertainment. As their parents, we strongly believe that it is our responsibility to help them forge a deep connection to the natural world. A world where time moves at its own pace, where an alpine lake invites you for a swim and an overnight stay in a mountain hut offers a window to a star covered sky.

Hiking, which is more than the kilometers we amble on meticulous trails, has provided our family with the opportunity to connect to a world that is full of possibilities and wonder. For us, there is no better landscape to teach our children valuable life lessons and to remind us, as humans, we need and thrive in the natural world. Switzerland is the perfect country to offer such possibilities.

For those of our readers who are familiar with our first book, *Fresh Air Kids Switzerland - 52 Inspiring Hikes That Will Make Kids and Parents Happy*, we are certain you have now witnessed the relentless magic of nature. We have returned to remind you that hiking with children is possible and can truly be a life enriching experience.

In this book, we share some of our favorite overnight and multi-day tours with you. As our own children advance in age and their once tiny legs grow stronger and more able, we are excited to expand day trips into overnight excursions. Hiking longer distances, experiencing deeper valleys and climbing higher mountains, has ultimately translated into grander family adventures.

In the pages that follow, we provide details on sleeping in mountain huts, spending a night on straw at a working farm and discovering new alpine playgrounds. Some of the places mentioned in this book are so remote that they are accessible only by foot or helicopter. Each location is unique, and every hike is special. Such remarkable locations offer the space to pull away from our hectic routines and the opportunity, as a family, to fall deeper into the Swiss landscape and each other.

We completed the legwork, worked out the details, and made the mistakes so that you, our reader, do not have to. We hiked each path and personally stayed in every accommodation recommended in the pages that follow. You can trust the routes outlined and search for your next weekend or vacation destination with ease.

Now it is time to turn this experience over to you. It is our hope that you witness the same sense of joy that has washed over us each time we step into the mountains.

Melinda & Robert

CHAPTER II

Mountain Ready — Know Before You Go

"

A perfect gift for anyone who loves the outdoors
is inviting them on an adventure.

"

BEN STOOKESBERRY
ADVENTURER

Books such as this require candid honesty. We must confide in you that the pages that follow were nearly scrapped and this project was almost abandoned before we had the chance to breathe life into its pages. Our children were coming off of a hectic school year; we were all exhausted from the demands of our routine schedules and naturally, our patience was on edge. The stamina required for such excursions was wavering.

One day, when we missed a train connection (the only train for hours), we stood on the platform of the station knowing that our day was about to stretch on hours and hours longer than anticipated. As we gazed down at our rambunctious children, we looked at each other, frustrated, exhausted from the sweltering heat and the weight of our backpacks. The hike, let alone the entire project, felt overwhelming. And on that very platform, with tears forming in our eyes we debated: board the first train back to our home town or wait the excruciating hours required to make our next connection via train, bus and ultimately, foot? The idea of unpacking our bags permanently was appealing. The notion of sleeping in our own beds was incredibly alluring and the thought of showering in a shower free of a coin dispenser, or a timer, was luxurious. But despite some of the comforts that lured us back, the reality was, that decision carried profound weight not only for us as parents, but for our children as well.

We have come to realize that persistence rewards you and, as parents, we didn't want to instill in our children the art of giving up; of merely throwing in the towel when trains were missed and the temperature rose. We didn't want to fall into the comfort of the familiar and miss the excitement of the unknown. After much deliberation, we elected to carry on because at the end of the day, we believe strongly in what we are doing.

Through our adventures we have come to fall into the calm of foreign beds that have rested many a weary body before us. We have fallen asleep under a star-filled sky and woken the next morning only to do it all over again. We created a simple rhythm of hiking, discovering, eating and sleeping. That pattern has filled our days with so much more than the ground we cover. Such days have imparted some of life's greatest lessons and deepest joys. Thus, we keep enduring and keep on exploring.

Hiking to huts does require more effort, slightly larger packs, a great deal of preparation and often fortitude. Despite the preparation and mental strength that is required, the reward of the journey and, ultimately, the arrival at your hut, is worth the effort. There is something intoxicating about hiking through remote valleys and perhaps being the only individuals on the trail. All of our senses are activated when we are outside and we feel alive in a way that doesn't exist for us in the city. These moments prove yet again that hiking isn't a complicated pastime, rather an activity that can afford families a multitude of benefits for those that are willing to cover the distance and step into the unknown.

In this chapter we share with you all those odd details that will help to ensure a successful hiking and overnight experience. We have forgotten a towel, made absurd mistakes too embarrassing to even mention and assumed lifts were running when they weren't. In this chapter we breakdown all the essentials so that you start your journey with the knowledge you need, the directions you require and the accommodations reserved in advance so that you can have a tremendous family experience.

Success on the Trail

What does it mean to hike to huts with children and what are multi-day tours?

Hikes to huts are hikes that lead to a mountain accommodation for an overnight stay. Unlike a typical hike, these routes may be longer in both time and kilometers and will lead to a specific destination, in this case, your sleeping quarters. These paths are typically, though not always, on white-red-white trails requiring general comfort with hiking and navigating mountain paths. Backpacks are typically larger, as you will need to carry a change of clothes, rain/warm weather gear, water, trail snacks, toiletries, sleep sacks, a towel, a medical kit and potentially a harness (we will provide a detailed list of what to pack in the pages to come).

Multi-day tours are hikes that lead you from one hut to another over the course of several days. These hikes require endurance and certainly more supplies. They may start at one location and end at a very different point.

Is it possible to hike to huts with children?

The quick answer is yes, it is absolutely possible to hike to overnight destinations with your children at your side and it can be a true pleasure. Our family, including our two children, completed all the hikes outlined in this book. We recommend this book for experienced hiking families and children that are old enough to hike without the need to be carried or pushed in a stroller.

We never promise easy, but your journey will be more manageable with adequate preparation (both mental and physical) and the right gear. The rest is up to you!

Steps to Take for Trail Safety

Step One – Not Stroller Friendly
The trails outlined in this book are not passable with a stroller. If you attempt to push your child in a stroller, you may be putting your child at risk. If you are still in the "stroller" phase of your parenting journey, we can recommend our first book, *Fresh Air Kids - 52 Inspiring Hikes That Will Make Kids and Parents Happy*, which includes hikes that are suitable for strollers.

Step Two – Experienced Hikers
The hikes outlined in this book are for experienced hiking families. That refers to those families that have spent time on trails, know how to read trail markers and have children that are accustomed to hiking. Families will be required to navigate narrow trails use handholds and cables on some routes, which we indicate on each overnight stay or tour accordingly. We rate all of the hikes according to an easy to follow system, outlined in the pages that follow.

All of the hikes in this book require good hiking boots for each family member and appropriate hiking clothes. Please remember that sneakers are not hiking boots and do not offer the tread or traction required for hiking on mountain trails. Always turn your hiking boots over to inspect the tread. If the tread is low, it is time for new shoes. Check the tread on your children's boots as well.

Step Three – Seasonal Hikes
The hikes outlined in this book are relatively seasonal (unless otherwise mentioned), meaning, the main hiking window for most mountain accommodations is from June through the end of September / early October depending on the elevation of the route and the location of the hut. The season will also be dependent on the snowfall. Some huts will not open until later in the season due to remaining snow levels and may close early due to the premature arrival of snow. Know this prior to starting your journey. Also, never attempt to hike in bad weather conditions and check forecasts before starting out.

There are a few routes listed in the book that are ideal for winter hiking. In those cases, we are clear with our description and huts should be open during the winter months, but always confirm opening times in advance.

Step Four – Confirm That Trails and Lifts Are Open

Always confirm that the chosen route is open and that the lifts you may need to rely on for transportation are operating. There is nothing worse than arriving at your destination only to discover that the trails are closed due to poor weather or snow levels. Lifts may also be closed if it is too early in the season or during the shoulder season. Local tourist information centers and local websites are helpful when determining whether or not trails are accessible.

Step Five – Reserve All Accommodations in Advance

Always, and we mean always, book your accommodations in advance. Due to the short season of the locations outlined in this book, booking your stay far in advance is not only advised, it is truly necessary (it is not uncommon for rooms and dormitories to reach full capacity one month prior to your arrival, especially on weekends). Private rooms, if available, are the first to be reserved. Don't miss out on incredible opportunities by waiting until the last minute to reserve your room or dormitory.

Never assume that space is available upon your arrival without a reservation.

Reservations may be made by calling the hut and in some cases, accommodations will accept reservations made online or via email. Please confirm all online reservations prior to your arrival. We have provided all contact details in this book for you.

Step Six – Pack and Wear Layers

Pack and wear layered clothing. Whenever venturing into the Alps, even in the summer months, layers are essential. There have been times when we have been wrapped in all of our layers in summer due to changing weather or elevation. Plan this in advance and look at our checklist for the perfect items to include in your backpack.

Step Seven – Food, Water and Cash

Bring food and water with you on each and every hike. Never rely on water being available on the trail. Pack enough for each person in the group for the duration of the hike and perhaps extra if the temperatures are high. Some of the huts mentioned in this book charge high prices for drinking water. The cost is due to the fact that the tap water at the hut may not be suitable for consumption; therefore, the drinking water must be brought in. Please just pay the cost of the water to remain adequately hydrated throughout your stay, which is essential when traveling in the Alps.

We recommend that you always travel with cash (some huts require cash) in the event you stumble upon mountain snacks for sale, either at a self-service kiosk or a mountain inn along the route. Having cash and change on hand is always a good idea when hiking in the Alps.

Step Eight – Adults = Necessary Alone Time

This is a tip for the parents or adults in the group. Find some time to be alone. We have now started a little tradition of taking an early morning stroll without our children. When they are either still snug in their beds, or busy with an in-room game, we steal away for a short moment alone outside. This helps us, as a couple to prepare for the day ahead and enjoy some much-needed quiet time. During this sweet time, we have the opportunity to plan the day in advance free of distraction and to hear the sounds of the natural world undisturbed by tiny voices.

Step Nine – Stock the Fridge

Stock your fridge before you go. There is nothing more inconvenient than arriving back home after a long weekend of hiking and having to run to the store to grab something to cook for dinner. Plan an easy to prepare meal in advance and enjoy relaxing upon your return.

Step Ten – Be Flexible

Trains will be missed, weather will change and children will have meltdowns (who are we kidding, adults may have meltdowns too), but that is all part of the experience. If you know that somedays are going to be less than perfect, you might, just might, be better prepared to handle those crazy moments when they occur. Simply breathe, know the moment is temporary, smile and hike on, or refer to chapter four, which is full of child-friendly activities.

Mountain Accommodations

Mountain accommodations (SAC/CAS huts, mountain houses/hotels, hostels, and farm stays) offer unique lodging in gorgeous settings. Sometimes, these mountain accommodations require genuine effort to get to, but upon arrival, they impart endless joy. They are peaceful locations that may be at the end of deep, oftentimes, remote valleys. They offer respite in a hectic world and they provide a deep sense of calm. Those who work at such establishments are dedicated employees and take pride in their work. Alpine life is not always easy and great effort goes into providing guests with a memorable experience. Sometimes provisions, such as food, supplies and trash removal are brought in and out by helicopter, which is a costly service. Guests are encouraged to observe this effort and respect all that goes into making mountain huts true havens in the Swiss Alps.

For us, mountain huts are windows to the past and they might just hold the key to our future. A future that is slow and simple and meant to be savored. We encourage our readers to share such experiences with those you love, as these locations are incredibly special.

Below we list what mountain accommodations typically offer their guests and what they may or may not include when it comes to overnight stays. We provide this list to prepare our readers in advance, allowing you to make the most of your overnight experience.

Types of Mountain Accommodations

Swiss Alpine Club (SAC, or CAS in French/Italian)

The Swiss Alpine Club accommodations were initially established to serve climbers with key access points to the surrounding peaks; however, hikers are welcome. Accommodations are basic and functional. They typically offer beds in dormitories and often serve fixed menus.

Mountain Inns / Mountain Houses / Mountain Huts (Berghotels, Berghäuser, Berggasthäuser)

Unlike SAC accommodations, these establishments are typically independently owned and operated with amenities varying depending on the location and the accessibility. Mountain inns may offer private rooms; however, they book-up quickly. Dormitory rooms, meals and shared bathroom facilities are typical. *Berghotels* may offer more amenities than a typical *Berghaus* or Mountain Inn, including linens and towels, but not always.

Hostels/Auberge

Simple accommodations are offered with either private or dormitory style rooms. Meals are served typically à la carte and a modest breakfast may be included in the room rate.

Farm Stays

These stays include overnights on working farms. Some farms offer very modest accommodations in barns, with the opportunity to sleep on hay or in the barn loft. Meals may or may not be served.

Mountain accommodations ARE typically:

+ modest and simple
+ historic and antiquated
+ in remote locations
+ often free of technology/services (i.e. Wi-Fi)
+ seasonally operated
+ staffed by hardworking, good people
+ conservative with water, electricity and food
+ part of an active farm
+ able to provide shared bathrooms and showers, if showers are available
+ dormitory accommodations with few private rooms, if any (*Matratzenlager* in German or *dortoirs* in French – think rows of bunk beds shared by strangers).
+ able to serve the food they can easily obtain. Meals are often simple and breakfast is typically bread, butter, jam and coffee, which may be included in the rate. Do not expect much more, but the reality is, food tastes delicious after hiking for hours on the trails. If you have special dietary needs, clarify those needs when booking your accommodations and again upon your arrival.

Mountain accommodations are NOT:

+ luxury accommodations (depending on your view of luxury)
+ always easy to get to
+ always able to offer running water, drinking water, flushing toilets, showers, or electricity
+ always able to provide linens for overnight accommodations, however, they may be available for rent
+ always able to accept credit cards, requiring you to pay in cash
+ always able to reimburse cancelled reservations

General Behavior

All mountain accommodations require a great deal of work to run and operate. Thus, respect is necessary when visiting such locations. We always appreciate visiting inns because guests are polite, gracious and tidy. When entering any accommodation, it is almost always required to remove your hiking boots and place them in the designated area. Most, but not all, locations offer house shoes that are to be worn inside, during your stay. If you prefer your own, pack them.

Many inns have set mealtimes, which must be observed. Ask the innkeepers at each hut if breakfast and dinner times are fixed. If so, please arrive on time to respect those preparing your morning or evening meals.

It has been our observation that many inns are now mandating sleep sacks for overnight stays. Some inns will provide them on a rental basis; however, we advise purchasing your own and carrying them with you. The same goes for towels.

If showers are available at the inn, please do not be surprised if they operate on a timer and must be turned on by placing a coin/token in a machine. These timed showers are a reminder that water is not an infinite resource and is a luxury in the mountains. They may also serve as a reminder that we do not need long showers in order to get clean.

Please leave common spaces, such as bathrooms, showers, meal areas and bedrooms clean upon your departure. Some huts may even require you to sweep out your room prior to departing.

When sleeping in close quarters with strangers, it is respectful to wear appropriate sleepwear, observe quiet hours and keep noise to a minimum. Many hikers will rise early to reach a particular summit and therefore, need a good night's rest.

Tips for Parents

- When sleeping in a *Matratzenlager* (literally translated as, "mattress room"), it is advised to place your children in the middle of the adults. This way, children can sleep snug next to their family and will not disturb sleeping strangers next to them.

- Bring a flashlight for using the toilet at night.

- Speak to children about the quiet hours of the hut, so they too respect the rules of the house.

- Please assist children in shower rooms, especially when they are coin operated.

- Please encourage your children to try new foods and not to waste the meal provided to them by the hut.

Gentle Steps

Switzerland has unprecedented beauty and it is our responsibility to maintain and protect its natural landscape. Whenever we are in nature, it is our duty as parents, caretakers, and/or guardians to model respect for the environment, animals and the land. Remember you are the teacher, so teach and guide well.

When in nature, respect the following:

Risks
Whenever in the mountains, it is important to remember to enter such environments with careful attention. The mountains and all that surrounds them are extremely powerful, and venturing into nature has inherent risks. Always be aware of falling rocks, avalanches, and changing weather conditions. If you have questions, members of the hotel staff or local tourist information centers are typically good resources to consult, as are chairlift and gondola operators. Due to climate change, the natural landscapes are subject to inconsistent weather conditions. We have witnessed first-hand, avalanches, rock falls, and unstable terrain, which have influenced trail routes. We have stayed in accommodations that have had to be rebuilt structurally due to extreme weather conditions. Be aware and always veer on the side of caution whenever in the Alps.

Animals
Do not feed animals on the trail. Trails will often have animals such as; sheep, goats and/or cows grazing in the area. If you come across cows, be aware that these animals may be extremely protective of their young. Use caution when walking near calves and provide them with ample space. In some areas, guard dogs may be used to protect the livestock. Please know these animals are working. Never attempt to pet or get too close to these dogs, as they are not our furry friends. To learn more about the herd or working dogs, please visit: www.protectiondestroupeaux.ch.

Farm/Alpine Culture and Mountain Huts
Farming is a significant part of Swiss alpine culture. Farmers are hard workers and deserve respect. Whenever crossing through farms and areas that provide grazing for livestock, respect the land, the animals and all that goes into the daily responsibilities of these farms.

Trails

Stay on the trails. They are designated walking zones. By leaving the trail, you risk becoming lost or injured, or causing harm to others, the environment and natural habitats.

Fences

You should always close fences and gates whenever passing through farms, pastures and open fields. Please be aware that some fences are electrified and can deliver a strong shock when touched. Please alert children to this and help them open and close fences (especially rope barriers) along the trails.

Comfort Level

Whenever in doubt regarding the safety of a trail, trust your instinct and walk away. It is better to appreciate the beauty of an area from afar, rather than enter into a situation that may be unsafe, especially when hiking with children.

Grilling

Whenever cooking with an open fire, be sure to do so safely. Always extinguish a fire in its entirety before departing a particular site. In addition, heed the advice of posted signs. If the year has been particularly dry, warnings may appear that it is not suitable to create a fire.

Weather and Snow Levels

Conditions can change quickly in the mountains. Never attempt alpine hikes in poor weather. It is essential to check weather forecasts before starting out on any hike. Always check snow levels prior to starting your journey, even in the summer months. Check with the staff at the hut, as they are familiar with weather patterns in that particular area.

If the previous winter received significant snowfall, some routes, and/or passes may be closed or may not be safe for hiking. It is advisable to check websites and/or webcams in the area to determine if snow is still present and trails are open and safe for hiking.

Trash

Throw garbage (apple cores, snack wrappers, lunch remains, etc.) away in designated trash bins. If there are no trash bins available, take your trash with you and dispose of it properly at a later time. Please do not spit chewing gum out on the trail. Know that trash left on the trails can harm or even kill animals and/or livestock. Please respect these creatures.

Some huts will require you to carry all of your trash with you, thus requiring you to bring your own bag to remove garbage.

Dogs

If you have a dog, be sure to clean up after the animal and keep your dog on a leash wherever posted. Some mountain accommodations permit dogs for overnight stays for a nominal fee. Determine dog policies prior to your arrival.

Flowers

Do not allow your children to pick flowers. They will wilt before you get back home and some flowers may be protected species.

Stinging Nettles – Ouch!

Stinging nettles may be abundant on the trails. If you or your child touches a stinging nettle, know that the antidote plant, dock weed (identifiable by its oblong shaped leaf and usually a red spine), typically grows in close proximity. Pick a leaf of dock weed, crush the leaf in your hands and rub it on the stinging area to minimize the pain. If you are unable to find dock weed, wash the area with cool water and try not to scratch your skin. Once you have access to soap, wash the area gently and place (by dabbing) a paste of baking soda and water on the affected area. Anti-itch cream may help too.

Hunting Season and Military Activity

Hunting in Switzerland is managed by individual cantons and typically occurs from September through December, and into February in some cases. Be aware that hunting is highly regulated and hunters are required to have extensive training before obtaining a license. Do not be surprised if you hear gunshots when hiking during these months. Also be aware, that there should be signs posted during this period in the area where hunting takes place. Information can be obtained from mountain accommodations or from the local municipality should you have any questions. Hunting should not be a deterrent from hiking, which can still be enjoyed safely during this season.

It is not uncommon for military activity to take place in remote mountain locations. The federal government recognizes the "coexistence" of the land for military and civilian use, and attempts to minimize downtime, however, passage in some areas may be restricted. Restrictions will be posted and mountain accommodations should be aware. It is extremely important not to touch any weapon ordnance if found on the trail, as it may be undetonated and/or toxic. More information can be found at: www.armee.ch/schiessanzeigen (available in German, French, and Italian). As a family that hikes often, we have only come across posted signs a few times.

Understanding Trail Markers

Individuals participating in hikes such as those outlined in this book, should feel comfortable in alpine environments and should know how to read trail markers/blazes. Listed below is a brief explanation.

 Yellow: Hiking Trails
Of all the hiking trails in Switzerland, the yellow trails are the easiest to navigate, however, that is not to say they may not require special attention to inherent risks. The yellow hiking paths are typically wide, but not always.

 White–Red–White: Mountain Trails
The majority of the hikes outlined in this book are on white-red-white trails. The Mountain Trails may be steep, narrow in some areas, and may include sharp drops or edges. Individuals hiking on these trails should be comfortable with their hiking abilities, and aware of potential rock and snowfalls. These trails often include steep ascents and descents. Handholds/chains may be present on these trails as a means to provide additional support and stability.

 White–Blue–White: Alpine Trails
Of all the trails, the Alpine Trails are those that often require a high level of hiking experience and mountaineering skills. Such trails may be at higher altitudes, over scree (loose stones), glaciers and rock with the potential need to use ropes, crampons, and other hiking equipment. These trails are potentially dangerous, requiring participants to hike and navigate at their own risk. These trails are best left for those who are comfortable taking risks and expert hikers.

 Pink: Winter Hiking Trails
These trails are designated as winter hiking paths for walking, snowshoeing, sledding and/or cross-country skiing.

The T Scale Classification

The T scale was created and put into place by the Swiss Alpine Club (SAC) in 2002. The T or "trekking" scale provides an overview of the terrain and the skill level required to hike on such routes along with basic guidance. As your skills progress, and as you venture further into Switzerland, it is important to be familiar with this scale, which is helpful when planning your own adventure. When unsure about a route, it is advisable to contact the location where you will be staying (or plan to stay) and ask for advice on the route.

T1 – Yellow Trails – General Hiking
The easiest of all hiking trails to navigate with flat or small slopes.

T2 – White/Red/White – Mountain Hiking
Requires basic skill level, some routes may be steep, and rock fall hazards are possible. Stability is required as are quality hiking boots.

T3 – White/Red/White – Challenging Mountain Hiking
Requires basic alpine experience, trails may be exposed in some areas with chains or handholds, which may be required to provide stabilization on these routes. Rocks and scree may be present on such routes, as are steep ascents and descents. Parents must feel comfortable assisting their children on these routes, and should consider the use of harnesses for smaller children. Good stability and balance are strongly advised, along with sturdy hiking boots.

T4 – White/Blue/White – Alpine Hiking
Good orientation needed as the trail is not always marked and the use of handholds may be needed to assist hikers. Terrain is quite exposed and may include scree and snow fields. It is recommended to have good alpine experience, with the ability to navigate and assess terrain, and sturdy hiking boots. T4 routes are not covered in this book.

T5 – White/Blue/White – Challenging Alpine Hiking
Very good orientation and alpine experience is advised to navigate terrain without a trail. Terrain includes challenging, exposed sections, steep crags, glacier and firn fields with the danger of slipping. Good alpine experience with axe and rope handling is advised. T5 routes are not covered in this book.

T6 – White/Blue/White–Mountaineering
Mature alpine experience, climbing exposed and tricky crags, familiarity with climbing equipment, and excellent orientation are a must on these routes. T6 routes are not covered in this book.

T4–T6 – These categories are perhaps too advanced for children and families in our opinion. Rest assured none of the hikes outlined in this book are on T4–T6 routes. Some routes in this book are T3, and may be too challenging for people with vertigo or with limited hiking experience. Always remember to hike at your own comfort level.

Yellow–Red Border Sign

The half yellow, half red border signs advise individuals of a wildlife-protected area. These border signs are posted to direct hikers to use extreme caution and consideration when passing through these areas.

Languages Used on Trail Markers

In each region, the trail markers will be labeled according to the local language. Be aware that this will vary according to the different locations within Switzerland.

How to Read Trail Markers

- The center of the trail markers, or the white section, lists your current position and elevation. The white middle section may not be present on all trail signs.

- Each town name or waypoint indicates the destination; often along with the estimated time it will take to reach that location from your current position without stopping. For example, "Riffelalp 2 h 10 min" means Riffelalp can be reached in roughly 2 hours and 10 minutes. Always allow extra time to reach the final destination when hiking with children. Our general rule is to double the indicated time on the trail marker, to allow for stops, refueling along the way and ample time to explore. Remember your children's steps will be smaller than your steps and children may tire quicker than adults.

- The names on the trail markers of destinations often include icons for a train, bus, and/or gondola stations. Those icons indicate that a specific mode of transportation is available at the end point. On occasion, the icon may be for a viewpoint, picnic spot, tourist information center or a restaurant.

- Some trail markers may not contain names. However, they may display a route logo or color codes. Such markers may indicate regional, local highlighted routes or theme trails.

- The yellow diamonds (with a person hiking, plain yellow, with words, canton emblem, etc.), as well as the white-red-white painted lines and white-blue-white painted lines along the trails are confirmation that you are on the right route.

- Trail markers may appear on trees, rocks, buildings, trash cans, poles, fences, or other objects along the route. Look for the trail markers as you hike to ensure you are on the correct route.

- Intermediate trail markers should be visible at regular intervals (30–70 m), at branches of the trail, or if the trail changes direction. If there is no opportunity to go off course (e.g. an unbroken path without cross-roads), the markers may be less frequent, up to 500–700 m apart.

Our hope is that the directions provided in this book serve as a reference and are not your only guide while hiking. You should feel comfortable reading and following trail markers.

Trail Maintenance, Trail Closures, Changes to Trails and Mountain Accommodations

It is quite possible that some of the trails mentioned in this book are either under maintenance, closed due to weather conditions or have changed over the course of time. Some of the mountain inns may also be under construction or closed due to changes in management or for other reasons. It is advised to always contact the mountain inn in which you hope to stay far in advance to ensure the accommodation is open and to secure your reservation prior to your arrival.

We have done our best to provide accurate information in this book. We apologize if the information provided is not correct and would like to hear from you should this be the case (info@helvetiq.ch). To determine if the route you have selected is currently open and safe for hiking, first check with your overnight accommodation or consult one of the following resources before starting your journey:

● Local tourist information centers
  (may show trail status for summer and winter activities)

● Switzerland Tourism – www.myswitzerland.com

● The Swiss Hiking Trail Federation – www.wandern.ch (DE) / www.randonner.ch (FR)

● The Swiss Alpine Club – www.sac-cas.ch

How to Use This Book

Trail Difficulty

We categorize all hikes and routes in this book as easy, moderate or challenging.

Easy
These hikes indicate that families can enjoy this route with minimal effort. The trails are relatively easy to navigate and do not require substantial effort.

Moderate
These hikes signify that the trail may be long in length, may require some uphill climbs or steep descents. They are certainly manageable for most individuals, but will require physical effort. Moderate hikes are great for families looking for some challenge without exerting too much mental or physical strain.

Challenging
These hikes deserve more time and more trail awareness. They may have steep ascents and descents or ridgelines, requiring more skill, concentration and general knowledge. Challenging hikes are not recommended for individuals that have vertigo and are not comfortable navigating steep hills, ridgelines or feel uncomfortable holding on to ropes/chains for additional support. Harnesses are often recommended for children on such routes. Hiking poles may also be useful.

Distance and Length of Hikes

We have done our best to accurately indicate the distance and time of each hike listed in the book. Please take all lengths and times as reasonable estimates. Times are based on our moving time and not total duration, therefore, stops, snacks, and breaks were not typically accounted for in our calculations.

Be aware that GPS tracking and smartphone apps are valuable tools, however, from our experience the positional accuracy and length of a route can vary significantly due to multiple factors.

Types of Hikes

Out-and-back
A route that returns you along the same path you hiked out on.

Point-to-point
The start point is different from the end point.

Loop
Starts and finishes in the same location taking you in a circular route.

Tour
A point-to-point, multi-day journey including more than one overnight accommodation. Tours can also be broken down as an individual overnight stay as well.

Transportation

Start/End Point
We have listed each start/end point as shown on the SBB.ch website. We indicate if the stop is a train, bus, etc. in parenthesis for each hike if this information is not explicit. If driving, know that all hikes start from a public transportation stop, a gondola, funicular, etc., however, we did try to identify parking locations when possible.

Buses
Hikes that rely on a bus for transportation may not be the best option on Sundays or holidays due to the infrequency in which the buses run. Some locations are so remote that buses may only provide transportation one time per day. Plan accordingly by viewing timetables before your departure. Additional note, if you or your child tends to get carsick on curvy roads, please be prepared for bus rides. Oftentimes, the roads in which they drive are full of switchbacks. Yikes!

Pictograms

Whenever you see a pictogram within chapter 3, the hike will include one or more of the special features listed below.

 UNESCO World Heritage Site

 Geology

 Boat Rental/ Fishing

 Animals

 Winter Options/ Snowshoeing

 Theme Trail

 Playgrounds

 Waterfall

 Glacier

 Flowers

 Lake

Each hiking excursion will include:

- **The name of the hut** and all contact details (which are subject to change)

- **The canton** – based on where the overnight accommodation is located

- **The trail difficulty** – we list all hikes as easy, moderate or challenging (all hikes in this book are on yellow or white-red-white trails)

- **Type of hike** – indicates if the hike is out-and-back point-to-point, a loop or a tour

- **The start point** – where the hike starts based on the public transportation stop

- **The end point** – where the hike ends based on the public transportation stop

- **The distance to the hut** – the kilometers required to hike to the overnight accommodation from the start point

- **Total distance** – the kilometers from the start point, to the accommodation, and to the end point

- **Approximate time to hut** – the reasonable time it took us from the start point, with our children, to hike to the overnight accommodation

- **Time away from hut** – the time it took us as a family to reach the end point

- **Total hiking time** – the combined time it took us to hike from the start point to the overnight accommodation and from the overnight accommodation to the end point

- **Hiking profile** – the hiking profile includes the distance, elevation and points along the route

- **Hut elevation and highest point** – the hut elevation indicates the altitude at the hut, while the highest point indicates the highest altitude of the entire hike

- **Overview** – is a brief synopsis of the hike

- **Directions** – an overview of how to get to and from the overnight accommodation(s)

- **Trail markers** – the waypoints for easy navigation along the route

Each overnight accommodation will include:

- **Months calendar bar** (when accommodations are open)

- **Wi-Fi access** (or not)

- **Level of cellular connectivity**

- **Showers** (when available) – are private, coin operated or shared

- **Bathrooms** – private, or shared

- **Vegetarian options** – are vegetarian options available

- **Heat/electricity** – does the accommodation offer heat/electricity

- **Dormitory or private rooms** – the type of accommodation to expect

- **Sleep sack required** (we recommend light weight sacks for ease of packing and carrying, though be aware that they provide little warmth)

- **Towel required**

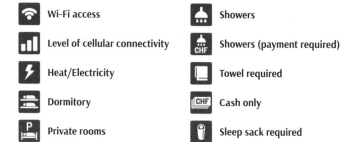

	Wi-Fi access		Showers
	Level of cellular connectivity		Showers (payment required)
	Heat/Electricity		Towel required
	Dormitory		Cash only
	Private rooms		Sleep sack required

If an icon does not appear, then it does not apply to the accommodation.

Please refer to individual websites for the cost of overnight accommodations, as prices may vary.

Tips

Tips will be provided for each and every route to make your journey more enjoyable.

Safety First

Hiking has inherent risks that must be assumed by all participants. Each individual is responsible for his or her own safety, and the safety of their children while on trails, near bodies of water and whenever in nature. Be responsible and safe.

As children grow and learn to hike more independently, it is important that they are educated on the importance of staying on the trail and know how to read a trail marker, as well as learn how to prevent falls and signal for help. Children should always stay within sight of adults or the trail leader whenever hiking. When crossing over dangerous or risky areas with children, either harness the child, or keep the child on the inside of the trail. Children should learn to carry their own backpack with water, snacks, a light jacket, a small first-aid kit and a whistle for safety purposes. If a child becomes lost on a trail, he or she should stay where they are and use the whistle to signal for help. By educating children on safety prior to starting out on your journey, you provide them with the knowledge and skills they require to hike with confidence.

Whenever hiking on unfamiliar trails, especially at higher elevations, it is advised to pack a harness or a rope for your child(ren). Despite the looks you may encounter, it is better to be safe than regretful. Know how to safely use a rope prior to hiking.

We assume no responsibility for individuals who read this book and participate in hikes outlined on the pages that follow.

In case of an emergency please remember the Rega emergency phone number 1414. To read more about Rega, please see chapter 4.

Equipment Check

What to Wear

Whenever hiking, wear comfortable, outdoor clothing. Hiking pants that dry quickly and zip off to become shorts are ideal, as are functional T-shirts and long sleeves. During the height of tick season, it is advised to wear long sleeves and pants in light colors. Individuals with long hair should keep their hair back and in a hat. It is strongly advised to always wear proper hiking boots with good tread. Please know that sneakers or tennis shoes are not a substitute for hiking boots. Hiking socks are recommended and make a difference when it comes to general comfort.

Clothing Check

What to pack for overnight stays and multi-day tours.

Always consider temperatures and snow levels when packing. The packing list depends on the amount of time you plan on hiking and the number of overnights required for the tour. Everyone in the group should carry his or her own backpack, keeping in mind that the more you pack, the harder it will be to climb up the mountains. If you don't mind wearing dirty T-shirts or your hiking pants multiple times, go for it!

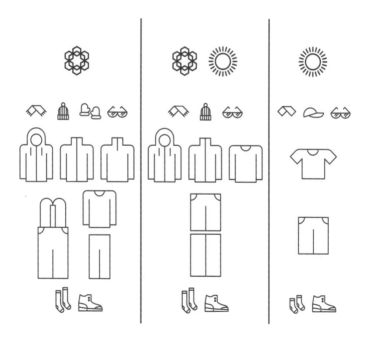

Hats

Sun hats or baseball caps are ideal to shield your face and eyes from the sun's intense rays, and winter hats offer protection from cold temperatures by providing an extra layer of warmth.

Scarves and Bandanas

These items can serve multiple purposes and come in handy in both hot and cold weather. On hot days, dip the bandana in water and wrap it around your head or neck to instantly cool the body. Scarves or bandanas can also be used as small towels to dry wet bodies or to provide warmth.

A change of clothes

Pack a clean shirt and underwear for each day on the trail. A long sleeve shirt and an extra pair of hiking pants may also be packed. Consider packing a change of clothes to wear to dinner, but this is not necessary. Children may require one extra change of clothes due to potential spills and accumulated dirt.

Waterproof clothes

When hiking in the Alps, be prepared for all types of weather. Weather can change without warning. Always pack an extra layer of warm clothing. Durable jackets, such as fleece, or down and/or rain jackets that can easily fold up, requiring very little space, are ideal for hiking. Also, consider rain pants if the forecast indicates rain. A small pair of gloves or mittens helps to keep hands warm when the temperatures fall and can be stored easily.

Pajamas

Remember you may be in a shared space with other people, so select wisely.

Socks for each day on the trail

(yes, to fresh socks).

Clothing Tip

Pack base layers: Long underwear and long sleeve shirts for children to sleep in. This way, if the weather turns cold, they can wear their "pajamas" as a base layer under their hiking clothes.

General Backpack Check

Sleep Sack

Some mountain accommodations may require a thin sleeping bag liner for overnight stays. We recommend sleep sacks with a built-in pillow case, as some mountain inns require pillowcases. Sometimes sleep sacks are available for rent, but check in advance. It is always advised to pack a sleep sack for each member of your group.

Towel

Some mountain accommodations offer towels for overnight stays, while others may not. Packing a small, quick-dry towel (one or two is sufficient for the entire group) is advisable and even comes in handy for alpine lake swims.

Hiking Poles

Some hikers appreciate the extra stability that poles provide when hiking. Pack poles for long treks, or for hikes that require a great deal of ascents and descents.

Plenty of Water

Water is essential for every hike, so either invest in a large hydration pack (water bladder) or a few quality water bottles that are sturdy and built to last. Each family member should have his or her own bottle of water that holds enough water for each journey from start to finish. Never rely on water being available along the trails. When hiking in the winter months, we recommend packing a hot tea, coffee or hot chocolate for the group, which is a great way to warm-up along the trail. Please note some mountain accommodations are not able to supply drinking water for a multitude of reasons. Water is available for purchase (be prepared to spend a lot of money for water) and some accommodations offer what they refer to as *Marschtee*, which is a homemade tea ideal for hiking. This is almost always free of charge and guests are welcome to fill their water bottles.

Sunglasses

Bring a pair of sunglasses for everyone in your group, especially if you plan to hike in winter and summer when the sun can be particularly intense and can reflect off water and/or snow.

Food and Treats

Pack plenty of food for each hike. Ideal food for hikes includes: fruit (fresh and dried), vegetables, olives, trail mix, hard-boiled eggs, crackers, cheese, granola bars, and sandwiches. For multi-day tours, pack food that doesn't require refrigeration. Having a special treat for your group can be the extra incentive you need to get your children through the last leg of what may be a long hike. Some mountain accommodations will provide you with a picnic lunch for a small fee if requested in advance.

Plastic Bags

Plastic bags are very helpful for soiled or wet clothing, but use conservatively. Old coffee bags that once housed whole coffee beans or ground coffee are great for carrying stinky trash, as they do an incredible job of masking nasty odors. Remember that the planet doesn't need more plastic waste, so do your best to use only what you need and dispose of waste properly.

Wet Wipes

Wet wipes serve multiple purposes, such as cleaning up spills, wiping dirty faces, refreshing armpits and cleaning hands. Pack plenty.

Knife

We cannot emphasize enough how often we use our multi-purpose Swiss Army knives when we hike. We cut fruit, remove splinters with the tweezers, saw wood, etc. If you do not have a multi-purpose knife, consider purchasing one. Pack a small knife for children as well. With proper instruction and supervision, children will enjoy whittling sticks.

Binoculars

These are handy for spotting animals and other hard-to-see objects in the distance. Children also enjoy searching the landscape with binoculars and may even want their own pair.

Flashlight/Nightlight

Having a flashlight, especially in those mountains accommodation that do not have electricity, is invaluable. Having a small nightlight to offer illumination in private rooms is also helpful when traveling with children.

Harness or Rope for Safety

We purchased a harness at a local store and always carry it with us whenever we are in a new hiking area or are unfamiliar with a particular trail. Our children do not like to wear their harnesses; however, our first priority as parents is their safety.

Phone/Camera/Power Bank

Do not forget to bring your camera. There is nothing more enjoyable than capturing your children in nature and creating a family photo album. You will reflect on these images for years to come. A cell phone may also be used as a safety tool should you receive cell service while on the trails. A power bank is essential for recharging your devices on overnight or multi-day tours, particularly if you are using GPS or hiking apps, which quickly drain your battery.

Wallet

Bring your travel passes (tram, train, Half Fare Travel Card, Junior Card, etc.), health insurance cards, your ID card, permit or photo identification. Always bring plenty of cash, as some mountain accommodations function on a cash only basis.

Half Fare Travel Card (Halbtax)

The SBB Half Fare train ticket is a phenomenal deal and worth the investment if you frequent trains and other modes of public transportation throughout the year. This card offers discounted transportation rates across Switzerland.

Junior Card

The SBB Junior Card is for children six-years of age and older when traveling with a parent. Children travel free of charge from six until their sixteenth birthday on most forms of transportation (within the half-fare travel zones) as long as the child is accompanied by his or her parent. To determine where the Junior Card is valid, simply visit the SBB website and download the "Synoptic Map."

Essentials to Pack:

+ All Toiletries (see below)
+ A Sleep Sack
+ A Small Towel
+ Ear Plugs
+ Phone and Power Bank
+ Cash
+ Medical Kit (see p. 49)

Toiletries:

+ Toothbrush
+ Toothpaste/Floss
+ Shampoo/Soap – Shampoo bars are ideal for travel.
+ Sunscreen – Trails are often exposed, which often means little to no shade leaving the skin vulnerable and subject to burns. Don't forget to pack plenty of sunscreen.
+ Lip Cream with SPF
+ Deodorant
+ Comb or brush (optional)
+ Tampons/Pads
+ Bug Repellent (especially tick spray)
+ Wet Wipes

Toiletry Tip: Ticks are quite the concern lately, as they are becoming more invasive and causing serious health concerns/problems. Even in the Alps it is necessary to take proper precautions. Wear protective clothing (long pants, high socks, long sleeves, pull back long hair and wear hats). Spray yourselves down with tick spray prior to starting your journey. A variety of tick sprays are available at all local pharmacies. You may choose the product that best suits your needs, but we prefer natural blends.

Always conduct a proper tick inspection of your children and yourself before retreating to bed in the evening. Remember that ticks navigate to warm places, such as, armpits, hair, behind the ears, neck, in the groin, and behind the knees.

Packing Tip: Reuse business class travel bags (those they give you for free on the airplanes) and use them as toiletry bags, a medical kit, or to help organize your belongings.

Medical Kit

Never leave home without having an adequately stocked first aid kit:

+ Pain reliever for both adults and children
+ Band-Aids in an array of sizes
+ Antiseptic spray
+ Insect repellent
+ Cream to help with insect bites and stings
+ Arnica cream for bruises
+ Arnica tablets
+ Gauze
+ Saline
+ Stomach medication
+ Tweezers
+ Eye drops
+ A small treat (candy, gum, a lollipop, etc.)
  to distract your child while you dress his or her wound.

Medical Kit Tip: Always bring headache medication when staying at higher elevations and drink plenty of water.

If you use supplies from your medical kit, restock the kit immediately upon your arrival back home. There is nothing worse than needing a medical supply only to discover that it was used on your last excursion.

Hiking Checklist

Always Check...

- O Weather/Forecast

- O Operating Times/Closures of Transportation
  (lifts, funiculars, gondolas, trains, buses, boats, etc.)

- O Snow Levels/Trail Closures

The Overnight Backpack Checklist:

- O This book or GPX files, plus access to transportation timetables

- O Hats for sun and warmth

- O Sunglasses

- O Rain gear/warm clothes

- O Scarves/gloves

- O A change of clothes (add an additional change of clothing, underwear and
  socks depending on the number of nights you are traveling)

- O Hiking poles

- O Towel(s)

- O Sleep sack(s)

- O Water

- O Food/Snacks

- O Wet wipes

- O Plastic bags

- O Medical kit

- O Flashlight

- O Binoculars

O Sunscreen

O Swiss Army Knife

O Harness or rope for safety

O Phone/camera/power bank (power banks are essential)

O Toiletry bag with all the essentials

O Wallet with all the essentials (bring additional cash depending on the number of nights you are traveling)

Helpful Resources

Swiss Tourism
Myswitzerland.com is a tremendous online resource, created by the National Tourist Information Organization. The site provides inspiration for numerous activities and locations throughout Switzerland. Detailed information on Switzerland's geography, customs, and history is also available on the site.

The Swiss Alpine Club
The Swiss Alpine Club, founded in 1863, released its SAC Tour Portal in 2018. This is an excellent tool for planning locations to visit, and provides details on SAC accommodations, routes with T scale classification, and access points. The portal also provides details on winter activities, such as ski and snowshoe tours, as well as other valuable resources. It is easy to navigate and search and is available in German, French, Italian, and English. www.sac-cas.ch

SwitzerlandMobility App
This free app provides detailed maps of Switzerland with over 65,000 km of hiking routes within the country. Winter and summer activities, transportation stops, points of interest, a compass and GPS are also included. For more information on this app and the services provided visit the website: www.schweizmobil.ch

SBB Mobile App
The SBB Mobile app is simple, user-friendly and permits ticket purchases, provides timetables and schedule changes, as well as general information. For more information on this app and the services provided visit the website: www.sbb.ch

Bergfex GmbH App
This free app provides topographical maps in Europe, allowing users to track and record outdoor activities, such as hiking, biking, running, etc. For more information on this app and the services provided visit the website: www.bergfex.com

Swisstopo App
This free app offers detailed maps of all locations in Switzerland. This app permits users the opportunity to record routes for hiking, cycling and snow sports, and more. One of the best features of this app is the ability to create/plan your own route by selecting points that the app will connect along the trail system. Visit the website for more information: www.swisstopo.ch

Rega Emergency Free App
Download the Rega emergency app, which can be used within Switzerland and just beyond the Swiss borders. This app is available for free and can be used should an emergency occur while hiking in the mountains. For more information on this app and the services provided visit the website: www.rega.ch

MeteoSwiss App

For weather in Switzerland, download the MeteoSwiss app. This app will show your position relative to weather in the area along with the forecast. For more information on this app and the services provided visit the website: www.meteoschweiz.admin.ch

Download the Hikes and Multi-Day Tours

For more information about the routes outlined in this book, download the GPX files from www.helvetiq.com prior to starting your adventure. GPX files can be uploaded to most hiking apps, although some apps may not import waypoints.

CHAPTER III

Into Fresh Air

“

Travel and change of place impart new vigor to the mind.

”

SENECA
PHILOSOPHER

We had to include the following lines because we thought it was important for you to know. We ran out of adjectives while creating this chapter. Yes, it is true. Switzerland is so absolutely beautiful that we did our best to verbally convey the stunning landscapes that make this country what it is, but there is a chance we may have failed. So, on the pages that follow you may grow weary of the words: beautiful, incredible, awe–inspiring, breathtaking, lovely, stunning, gorgeous, amazing, remarkable, magnificent, astounding, astonishing, incomprehensible, majestic, striking – did we miss any?

Please know we did our best and the only way to combat this overuse is for you to step outside and into this country that truly represents heaven on earth, and then perhaps you will understand our conundrum. Thank you for your patience and by all means, keep exploring and sharing nature with those you love; you may even come up with additional adjectives.

| J | F | M | A | M | J | J | A | S | O | N | D |

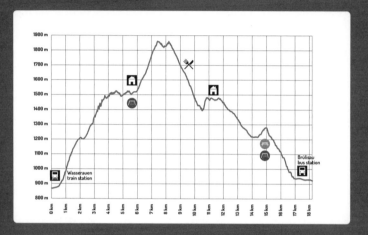

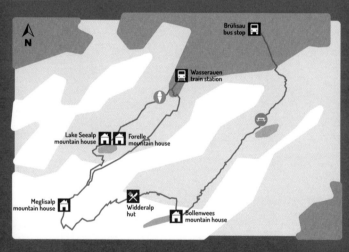

🪑 Picnic / Grilling

🎪 Playground

🍦 Ice cream

AI
BERGGASTHAUS MEGLISALP / BERGGASTHAUS BOLLENWEES

The Grand Tour of Appenzell

1

START	FINISH
Wasserauen, Station	**Brülisau, Kastenbahn**
(train station)	*(bus stop)*

1517 m		1369 m	1312 m	1864 m	T3
1471 m	18.4 km				

Day 1		Day 2		Day 3	
6.2 km	2:50 h	5 km	3 h	7.2 km	2:10 h
781 m	132 m	498 m	538 m	90 m	642 m

Berggasthaus Meglisalp

Berggasthaus Bollenwees

Overview

This gorgeous tour for intrepid hikers is a visual wonder throughout. Rich with lakes, farm animals and awe-inspiring views, the days spent on these trails will be a true pleasure.

As you arrive at Meglisalp sweaty and tired, it is quite possible you will receive a warm welcome from a resident cow or goat, making the experience that much more memorable. Check in to your room or dormitories, shower off the day's perspiration, pull up a chair and slowly eat a delicious, well-deserved meal. Once you are satiated, head outside once again to take in the night sky. Retreat to your sleeping quarters in time to get adequate sleep, preparing for the hike that awaits as the sun comes up.

The next morning another gorgeous day of unobstructed views is in store. Make your way to Bollenwees, where the trail continues to offer splendid views. Rest assured, if you like to push yourself, your wish will be fulfilled on this route. The children will enjoy the animals at farm Widderalp, which include pigs, chickens, cows and goats. The end of the day finishes with a nice clamber up to Fählensee. Reward yourself with a refreshing dip in the lake, check in to the *Berghaus* and get ready for yet another hearty evening meal.

The following day, the hike down to Brülisau starts out flat and relatively easy; a welcome reprieve from the last two days of climbing. As the hike continues, the descent will become steeper. Pace yourself and your children, as this route is wide but lined with gravel and loose stones. Once at Brülisau, wait to board the bus and make your way back home reflecting on three memorable days.

Directions

Day 1 — (Option 1 – moderate/T2)

From the Wasserauen train station parking lot, follow the signs toward Klein-Hütten. The trail will turn left when the trail splits just after Gasthaus Alpenrose. This is one of the two routes to Meglisalp. It is the route used for livestock, and recommend for groups with less hiking experience. This trail will zig-zag up through the forest and level off at Klein-Hütten. From there, keep left following signs toward Meglisalp. There are expansive views on this route, so stop to look around. Meglisalp will come into view during the last kilometer.

Day 1 — (Option 2 – challenging/T3)

This second option is an easier start, but may be challenging for those with less alpine experience after the lake (Seealpsee). This more challenging route from Wasserauen to Meglisalp takes you up to Seealpsee via a paved road. Follow the trail left at the end of the lake where the climb really begins. This next section contains multiple switchbacks and, after the forest, becomes exposed with narrow pathways and rope/chains for handholds. Once the switchbacks end, the trail will continue along a narrow path before emerging upon grassy slopes. Meglisalp is another 1.3 km ahead.

Day 2

Follow the signs in front of Meglisalp towards Widderalpsattel. The trail will zig-zag up grassy slopes for the first kilometer. This is where some of our favorite views come into sight. Continue uphill; the path soon levels and curves around towards Widderalp-sattel via a scree field. Keep a look out for ibex and chamois! Once over the pass, you will descend on Widderalp, which serves drinks and snacks. The trail will continue to descend, but stop and take in the dramatic mountain views as you keep right toward Bollenwees. At the next sign, you will turn right again, which takes you up a narrow gorge. This is actually an old fault line that runs through the area. Bollenwees is only 0.5 km away, just in front of the picturesque Fählensee.

Day 3

From Bollenwees, follow the trail towards Furgglen/Brülisau. Although this trail follows the road and appears easier than the previous days, it is longer. The trail will descend towards Sämtisersee through pastures, and after the lake, climb uphill to Plattenbödeli. Relax at the *Berggasthaus* before continuing. The trail will jump into the forest, on your left just after the *Berggasthaus*, and will continue down the road which will be steep at times. The road emerges at a parking lot and the path will continue along the road for another 1.3 km until the Brülisau, Kastenbahn bus stop.

Trail Markers

Day 1
Option 1 (moderate): Wasserauen » Meglisalp
Option 2 (challenging): Wasserauen » Chobel » Seealpsee » Meglisalp

Day 2
Meglisalp » Spitzigstein » Widderalpsattel » Widderalp » Bollenwees

Day 3
Bollenwees » Furgglen » Plattenbödeli » Pfannenstiel » Brülisau

Accommodation Overview for Berggasthaus Meglisalp

Staying in Meglisalp is like returning to the days of the past. The house is warm and welcoming and the rooms are cozy and clean. The dining room is bustling with activity and the evening meal is a true culinary delight. The staff is friendly and the location is picturesque in every sense of the word. We felt a pang of sadness wash over us when we left Meglisalp.

Did you know there was a plan to install the Säntis funicular and a stop at Meglisalp? It was originally started in 1912, but the First World War interrupted its construction. You can find the plaque and part of the plans posted on the side of the building next to Berggasthaus Meglisalp. As much as you could use the help climbing up, the railway would have changed the face of Meglisalp and sacrificed its charm in the process.

Meglisalp Details

Berggasthaus Meglisalp
9057 Weissbad / info@meglisalp.ch / +41 71 799 11 28
www.meglisalp.ch / GPS: 47.25577, 9.38549

+ Private rooms and dormitories
+ Shared bathrooms and showers, which are token operated
+ Electricity and outlets in the rooms
+ No Wi-Fi
+ Weak cellular connectivity
+ À la carte menu. Vegetarian options available
+ Cash and credit cards accepted

Accommodation Overview
for Berggasthaus Bollenwees

What makes Bollenwees spectacular is the lake. Arriving at Fählensee, you cannot help but reach for your camera. The lake is breathtaking and will invite you for a swim. Bollenwees has a lively vibe with some guests stopping in just for meals, while others will appreciate the house for the evening. The warmth of the dining area and the atmosphere encourage you to linger and reminisce about your day.

For more dramatic views of the mountains in the area, hike up to Saxerlücke, approximately a 2 km round trip from Berggasthaus Bollenwees. Use caution if hiking with children.

Bollenwees Details

Berggasthaus Bollenwees
9058 Brülisau / info@bollenwees.ch / +41 71 799 11 70
www.bollenwees.ch / GPS: 47.25305, 9.42462

+ Private rooms and dormitories
+ Shared bathrooms and showers for a fee
  Towels available for rent
+ Electricity and outlets in the rooms
+ No Wi-Fi
+ Good cellular connectivity
+ À la carte menu. Vegetarian options available
+ Cash and credit cards accepted

For those interested in extending the tour and comfortable with option 2, make Seealpsee your hub for the first night, allowing more time to linger at the lake and rest before making your way up to Meglisalp. In the event you wish to stay overnight at Seealpsee, there are two accommodations available on the lake listed below. We have personally stayed at both.

Other Mountain Houses on the Trail

Berggasthaus Forelle on Seealpsee
9057 Wasserauen / www.gasthausforelle.ch / +41 71 799 11 88

Berggasthaus Seealpsee
9057 Wasserauen / www.seealpsee.ch / +41 71 799 11 40

Kid Approved

+ The lake at Seealpsee (should you select option 2)
  is picturesque and will warrant time to play.
+ The small playground and working farm at Meglisalp
  with goats and cows are certainly a delight for children.
+ The animals and modest restaurant at Widderalp.
+ Fählensee (lake) at Bollenwees is gorgeous.

Tips

Tessa
If there is a cable on the hike, hold on to the cable.

Noah
Watch out for cow poop on the trail – it is hard to get off your shoes.

Parents
We highly recommend the macaroni with apple sauce and a local beer at Meglisalp, which were delicious!

Special Features

+ This tour provides incredible views throughout
  the three-day excursion.
+ This tour can be broken up by staying at Seealpsee,
  Meglisalp and Bollenwees.
  We elected to stay overnight at Meglisalp and Bollenwees.
+ There are two gorgeous lakes to offer reprieve from summer heat.
+ Rich farm life experiences are available
  for the children along this route.
+ A small playground is onsite for the children
  at Meglisalp and Plattenbödeli.

Be Aware

+ This tour is physically demanding.
+ If you select option 2, families must be comfortable with handholds/
  cables and navigating narrow/steep trails up to Meglisalp. Harnesses
  for children may be helpful on this route.
+ A great deal of ascents for the family
  to navigate the first two days of the tour.
+ Never attempt this hike in poor weather or rain.
+ This hike is best left for physically fit, experienced hikers.
+ Meglisalp was scheduled to undergo renovations and a building
  expansion in 2020.

J F M A M J J A S O N D

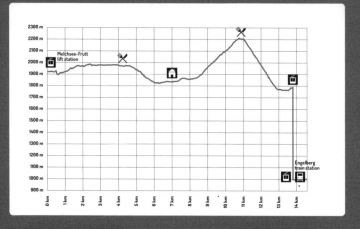

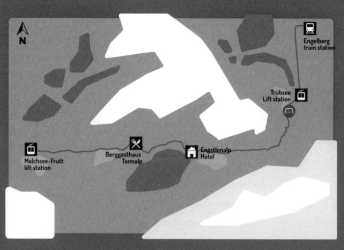

Playground

Swiss Bliss

START
Melchsee–Frutt, Bergstation
(lift station)

FINISH
Engelberg
(train station)

| 1839 m | 14.6 km | 616 m | 755 m | 2209 m | T2 |

7.1 km	3:30 h	7.5 km	3:15 h
Day 1		**Day 2**	
178 m	273 m	438 m	482 m

Hotel
Engstlenalp

Overview

This four-lake-one-pass hike is a beautiful experience during the summer and early autumn months. With clear lakes and activities to engage the children throughout, this route may quickly become a family favorite. The lakes provide refuge in the summer heat and there are plenty of inviting opportunities to picnic/grill.

Upon your arrival at Engstlenalp, you will feel as though you stepped back in time in such a wonderfully enchanting way. The evening meal is an elegant affair with dinner served on delicate dishes and appetizing smells that fill the room. Play a game as you relax around the table or allow conversation to carry you into the night.

After a peaceful night's sleep, enjoy a buffet breakfast before heading out for another day that is a feast for the eyes. Climbing over Jochpass and hiking down to Trübsee will reward you with views that will beg you to pull your camera out as you try to capture the marvelous scenery. Once at Trübsee, the children will want to spend hours playing at the creatively constructed "Schmuggler and Säumer" playground on the shore of the lake. A gondola is within short walking distance from the play area, which is available to sweep you down the mountain to Engelberg where the train station is in close proximity.

Directions

Day 1
Exit the Melchsee-Frutt Bergstation lift station bearing left in the direction of Tannenalp. The trail will turn left at Hotel Frutt Lodge. You can make your way down to Melchsee via the Panoramalift. Turn left, when facing the lake, and continue up through fields toward Tannenalp. Go past the Tannen lake dam along the road to Tannenalp. Arriving in Tannenalp, the trail turns right. You will pass a *Käserei* on your left, and the trail will continue through a field and begin to descend. The path will zig-zag; use caution here as the trail becomes narrow for about 150 m. Engstlenalp (and the third lake, Engstlensee) should be visible in the distance.

Day 2
From Engstlenalp, follow the trail on the right-hand side away from Hotel Engstlenalp (when facing the front of the Hotel) towards Jochpass. The trail will continue past Engstlensee and begin to zig-zag up to the pass. Note: In the early season when snow covers Jochpass, the lift at the back of Engstlensee should still be running but check in advance. At Jochpass, make your way down to Trübsee. In the summer, mountain bikes may share the start of this section. The hiking trail on this section is on a north-facing mountain, so there may be snow covering portions of the trail well into July depending on the winter snowfall. The descent covers approximately 2.2 km until the playground at Trübsee. Follow the trail to the Trübsee lift station, taking the gondola down to Engelberg. From the Engelberg lift station, the path to the train station crosses the river and passes a large parking lot. The train station is behind a row of buildings across the main street (Engelbergerstrasse).

Trail Markers

Day 1
Melchsee-Frutt >> Tannen Damm >> Tannenalp >> Engstlenalp

Day 2
Engstlenalp >> Jochpass >> Trübsee >> Engelberg (via lift at Trübsee)

Accommodation Overview

This delightful hotel that dates back to 1892, provides the opportunity to step back into simpler times. With antique rooms and a dining room that encourages you to linger, you will thoroughly enjoy this peaceful overnight destination surrounded by nature.

Acommondation Details

Hotel Engstlenalp
3860 Meiringen / hotel@engstlenalp.ch / +41 33 975 11 61
www.engstlenalp.ch / GPS: 46.77621, 8.34453

+ Private rooms and dormitories
+ Shared bathrooms and coin operated showers
+ Heat in the rooms
+ Electricity and outlets in the room
+ No Wi-Fi
+ Weak cellular connectivity
+ Fixed menu. Vegetarian options available, request at the time of booking
+ Only cash, Maestro and Post credit cards accepted

Kid Approved

+ The theme trail "Fruttli" at Frutt Lodge
  (plan roughly 1 h and additional 3 km to the overall hiking route.)
+ The Fruttli train from Melchsee-Frutt to Tannalp is perfect for tired legs.
+ The incredible "Schmuggler and Säumer" playground at Trübsee.

Tips

Noah
If you put your hiking boots in one of the lakes, they will probably stay wet for the rest of your hiking trip. Don't get your boots wet.

Parents
Never underestimate the power of a snowy winter. We made the silly mistake (despite knowing better) of trying to complete this hike in late June. We highly recommend completing this route later in the season when the snow has melted and the paths are easier to navigate, especially with children! When in doubt, check the lift webcams. June may be too early for this route, especially when crossing Jochpass at 2,209 m. Prior to starting out on this hike, confirm that the trail in its entirety is open, the pass is clear of snow and the lifts are running. Having the lifts to rely on can be helpful when traveling with children.

Special Features

+ There are four lakes along this route,
  providing opportunities to fish and swim.
+ The Engstlenalp Hotel is historic and charming.
+ Plenty of food, water and toilets are available
  at the hotels/mountain houses along the route.
+ This hike can be completed in reverse and can be made into a multi-
  day tour by staying in Melchsee-Frutt, Engstlenalp, Trübsee and
  perhaps even Engelberg.
+ There is a small dairy farm at Tannalp that makes cheese,
  butter and yogurt. Pop in for an educational experience!
+ Boats are available for rent at Trübsee.
+ The lift up to Melchsee-Frutt accepts *Halbtax* and the Junior Card.
  For more info, visit www.melchsee-frutt.ch. The lift down to Engelberg
  accepts the *Halbtax* and the Junior Card. For more info,
  visit www.engelberg.ch

Be Aware

+ Snow is possible in the early season (June and even July) depending
  on snow levels of the previous winter. Always check trail closures
  and lift information before booking your journey. From Jochpass to
  Trübsee the trail is north facing and snow may be present into July.
+ A chair lift from Engstlensee to Jochpass is seasonally available.
+ A bus is available from Engstlenalp in the event of inclement weather.
  Plan accordingly.
+ Poles may be helpful on this route.
+ Harnesses for children may be helpful, as there is one section after
  Tannalp with a chain hold and a narrow path.
+ Water is not available from Engstlenalp until Jochpass. Bring plenty.
+ Book the Hotel Engstlenalp far in advance.
+ Though the hotel is open in winter (based on their personal schedule)
  we do not recommend this route for families during the winter
  months.

J F M A M J J A S O N D

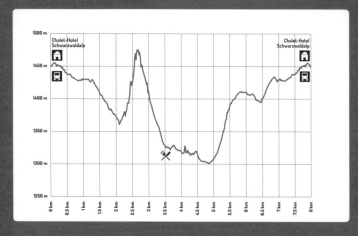

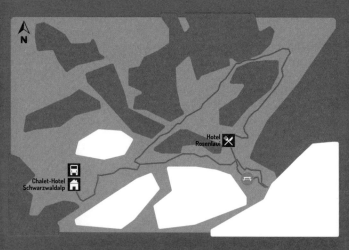

Picnic / Grilling

BE
CHALET-HOTEL SCHWARZWALDALP

Schwarzwaldalp and the Rosenlaui Gorge

3

START
Schwarzwaldalp
(bus stop)

FINISH
Schwarzwaldalp
(bus stop)

1455 m	8 km	1477 m	T1
589 m	3:15 h	590 m	

Chalet–Hotel
Schwarzwaldalp

Overview

This serene location offers peace and quiet for those looking to disconnect. This area is tucked deep in the back of the Rosenlaui Valley and offers an array of activities for the entire family. The Rosenlaui Gorge is part of the hike taking you up and through this hollowed, impressive area. Once across the valley, the Rosenlaui Glacier will come into view.

Spread across a green pasture, you will notice modest chalets, each with an incredible view of their own. The landscapes throughout this easy hike are alluring, encouraging you to take your time. Continue the hike to the back of the valley and through open meadows, which will lead you directly to your overnight accommodation at Chalet-Hotel Schwarzwaldalp.

Directions

After dropping your bags off at the Chalet-Hotel Schwarzwaldalp, follow signs toward Rosenlaui. The trail will head away from Hotel Schwarzwaldalp, up the road, and past a few small buildings. The trail will fork at one of the hotel buildings and continue through a field. Just after the small bridge turn left, continuing toward Rosenlaui. The trail will continue along the river heading downstream. The trail will deviate right, then left toward the main road and will make another right along the road. Continue along the road for approximately one kilometer until the Glescherschlucht. Here you will see the entrance to the Rosenlaui Gorge (Glescherschlucht). A visit to the gorge shows beautifully sculpted rock, cut over the centuries by the melt water of the Rosenlaui Glacier. A hike through the gorge and back down is approximately 1.2 km. From the gorge, the route will continue by crossing the street and will head toward the historic Rosenlaui Hotel. At the hotel, turn right, continuing down the road toward Gschwantenmad. The trail will almost immediately veer right, cross the stream again, and continue downstream. This will continue for approximately one kilometer before turning left at Gschwantenmad, crossing a bridge and then crossing the main road. At Gschwantenmad, stop for a moment and look back. The Rosenlaui Glacier and the mountainous backdrop is sure to impress. Once across the road, begin to head uphill through the small patch of historic farm houses. The trail will cross the road twice before heading through a narrow valley. Use caution at the top of the hill the trail will again come to the road and cross over. In 200 m, the trail will deviate left through a field toward Schwarzwaldalp. The trail will cross the road (and a bridge) at Broch, turning right at the end of the bridge, and then continuing upstream back to Schwarzwaldalp.

Trail Markers

Schwarzwaldalp ❭❭ Broch ❭❭ Gletscherschlucht ❭❭Rosenlaui ❭❭ Gschwantenmad ❭❭ Rufenen ❭❭ Broch ❭❭ Schwarzwaldalp

Accommodation Overview

This chalet, built in 1942, is located in a remote setting, despite the close proximity of the parking lot and the bus stop. Towering behind the hotel is the impressive wall of the Wetterhorn mountain.

The rooms are simple and the chalet is immaculate. The three-course dinner is served in the intimate dining room. The sound of cow bells and the small stream located behind the dormitory house might just lull you to sleep after a long day on the trails. The modest playground located at the chalet is a welcome treat for children. The neighboring sawmill, dating back 100 years, is both historical and educational and well worth a visit.

Acommondation Details

Chalet-Hotel Schwarzwaldalp
3860 Meiringen / info@schwarzwaldalp.ch / +41 33 971 35 15
www.schwarzwaldalp.ch / GPS: 46.67564, 8.13399

+ Private rooms with sheets, duvets and towels provided
+ Shared bathroom and showers
+ Heat in the rooms
+ Electricity and outlets in the room
+ No Wi-Fi
+ Moderate cellular connectivity
+ Vegetarian options available, request at the time of booking
+ Cash and credit cards accepted

Kid Approved

+ The opportunity to walk through the gorge is impressive.
+ The old sawmill; when staffed, the workers will happily give you a tour of the facility.
+ The tiny play area at the chalet.

Tip

Parents
Take the time to visit the old sawmill and witness history first-hand. Children will be fascinated by how the process of cutting wood the "old-fashioned" way works, and will walk away having gained valuable knowledge. Those that work at the sawmill are so delighted to have visitors and are more than happy to share the mill's history with you.

Special Features

+ This is a remote, natural location rich with beautiful views.
+ There are lots of additional hiking trails in the area.
  Get ready to explore!
+ The Rosenlaui Gorge and the Rosenlaui Glacier are gorgeous.
+ The bus ride up the valley is quite entertaining
  when the bus blows its horn.
  To us it sounds like "Schwarz-wald-alp."
+ The Hotel-Chalet Schwarzwaldalp sells local cheese onsite. Yum!
+ The trail overlaps with part of the Via Alpina
  and the Mountain Acorn Trail (Bergahornweg).

Be Aware

+ The Rosenlaui Gorge is a UNESCO
  World Heritage Jungfrau-Aletsch site.
+ The gorge is open daily from 09:00–18:00
  starting the end of May until the end of October.
+ Always wear appropriate shoes when visiting a gorge.
+ There is an entry fee to tour the Rosenlaui Gorge. Upon entering,
  ask for the "Guide through the Rosenlaui Gorge" informational
  brochure.
+ There is a toilet at the gorge, however,
  no water is available along the route.
+ The bus ride up is quite meandering,
  be prepared if you or your child is prone to carsickness.
+ We do not recommend this route during the winter months.

J F M A M J J A S O N D

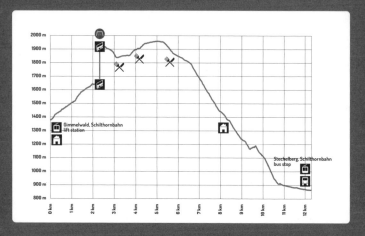

Gimmelwald, Schilthornbahn lift station

Stechelberg, Schilthornbahn bus stop

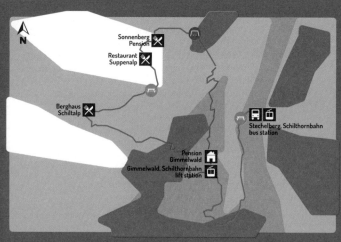

N

Sonnenberg Pension

Restaurant Suppenalp

Berghaus Schiltalp

Stechelberg, Schilthornbahn bus station

Pension Gimmelwald

Gimmelwald, Schilthornbahn lift station

Picnic / Grilling

Playground

BE
HOTEL PENSION GIMMELWALD

The Northface Trail

4

START
Gimmelwald, Schilthornbahn
(lift station)

FINISH
Stechelberg, Schilthornbahn
(bus stop)

1367 m	12.5 km	489 m	1260 m	1958 m	T2

8.5 km	3:45 h		4 km	2 h
Day 1			**Day 2**	
445 m	705 m		44 m	555 m

Hotel Pension
Gimmelwald

Overview

The Northface trail will make it obvious why hiking is such an addicting leisure activity in Switzerland. With incredible views throughout, including the visible faces of some of the famous Bernese Alps, you will need to keep your camera available. Lush green landscapes and a blanket of wild flowers in the early summer months extend for kilometers, making this a long, but visually appealing day on the trail.

Start at the Allmendhubel Flower Park and allow the children sufficient time to play. As they explore, this is your time to enjoy a coffee on the terrace at the Allmendhubel Bergrestaurant. Trails such as this should never be rushed. Simply stroll along and marvel at all the gorgeous views before arriving at the Hotel Pension Gimmelwald.

Directions

Day 1
Exit the Gimmelwald lift station, follow the road uphill, the playground will be on your left. Hotel Pension Gimmelwald will be on your left, on a corner approximately 100 m from the lift station. Drop your bags off at the hotel before beginning your journey, but remember to carry the essentials with you. Turn right, away from the hotel, following signs uphill to Mürren. The trail will zig-zag uphill, on and off a road at times. You will pass the Mürren Schilthornbahn and continue to the Mürren Allmendhubelbahn (funicular). Take the funicular to the top. Follow the signs toward Bluemental, past Höhlücke. The trail will turn right toward Im Suppen. The trail will head uphill, continue past Restaurant Suppenalp toward Im Schilt. The trail at Im Schilt will turn left and continue downhill along a mountain road. The trail will turn right just past a lift station, directing you toward Gimmelwald. This section is steep and will zig-zag back down to Gimmelwald. The trail will cross several roads and then merge onto a road; approximately 40 m ahead, you will see another set of trail markers with the Hotel Pension Gimmelwald next to them.

Day 2
You have the option to return to Stechelberg via the lift station, or to hike down. To hike down, follow signs toward Stechelberg/Wasserbrigg. From Wasserbrigg, keep left at each trail marker, ultimately following signs to Stechelberg. Once you are across the river from the lower lift station of Stechelberg, cross the footbridge over the river; there is a bus stop and parking lot at the lift station.

Trail Markers

Day 1
Gimmelwald **»** Mürren **»** Allmendhubel (via funicular) **»** Höhlücke **»** Bluemental **»** Im Suppen **»** Im Schilt **»** Gimmelwald

Day 2
Gimmelwald **»** Wasserbrigg **»** Schwendiwald **»** Schilthornbahn

Accommodation Overview

The Hotel Pension Gimmelwald is a 100-year-old rustic accommodation in the charmingly tiny, car-free village of Gimmelwald. The hotel offers a relaxed atmosphere and no shortage of good music. Sit on the terrace, enjoy a Schwarz Mönch beer (brewed by the innkeepers) and take in the views. The town is so quiet and peaceful you will feel a true sense of relaxation here.

Innkeepers Sabine and David and their two children make your stay with children relaxing. With plenty of games to play and delicious meals, you will feel quite content to retreat to the dining/living room to read a book by the fire, pull out your favorite game and sink into one of the sofas or cozy armchairs. Once you have had your fill of delicious food and music, make your way up to your room for a peaceful night's slumber. When you wake, visit the honesty shop for a quick souvenir before heading down the mountain.

Acommondation Details

Hotel Pension Gimmelwald
3826 Gimmelwald / welcome@hotel-pensiongimmelwald.ch / +41 33 855 17 30
www.hotel-pensiongimmelwald.ch / GPS: 46.5467, 7.89247

+ Private rooms with sheets, duvets and towels
+ Each room has a private shower and toilet located down the hall
+ Heat in the room
+ Electricity and outlets in the room
+ Free Wi-Fi
+ Good cellular connectivity
+ Fixed menu. Vegetarian meals available, book in advance
+ Cash and credit cards accepted

Kid Approved

+ The Flower Park playground at Allmendbubel is a true gem!

Tip

Parents
The hike on the Northface trail can be made easier by dropping off your backpack at the Hotel Pension Gimmelwald and carrying only the essentials.

To return to Stechelberg, consider hiking down from Gimmelwald, which is a descent hike that passes forests and waterfalls and can be completed in roughly two hours or 4 km. Follow signs to Stechelberg and then to Schilthornbahn. This provides the opportunity for the group to get some fresh air before sitting in the car or the train for the ride home!

Special Features

+ This hike offers dramatic views throughout.
+ The Allmendhubel Flower Park is a huge hit with the children.
+ Plenty of Berghotels to stop for a rest, a meal, or the toilet.
  (Allmendhubel, Sonnenberg, Suppenalp, Shiltalp).
+ Unprecedented beauty offering views of the north faces
  of the famous mountain peaks in the Bernese Alps.
+ Information boards along the route to educate you
  about the mountains.
+ The lifts in the area accept *Halbtax* and the Junior Cards.
  For more information visit: www.schilthorn.ch

Be Aware

+ Due to the elevation of this route,
  check the weather before starting off and pack layers.
+ This is a long day out. Be prepared with plenty of water,
  snacks and games!
+ Use caution when hiking through cow pastures,
  especially when calves are present.
+ Be aware of the descents, which are typically hard
  on the toes and knees. Poles are advised.
+ This hike is not advised, nor open during the winter months.
  This route is typically accessible May through October; however,
  determine trail access before starting out.
+ The pension is open year-round, though always check
  the website or with the owners for any closures.

J	F	M	A	M	J	J	A	S	O	N	D

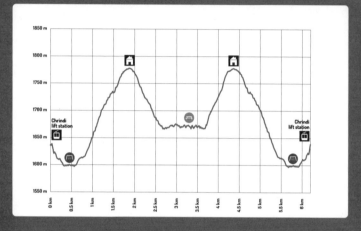

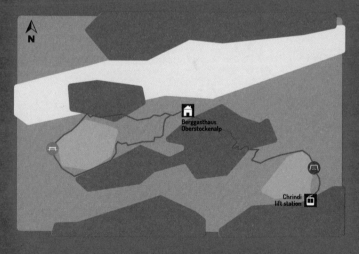

Berggasthaus
Oberstockenalp

Chrindi
lift station

Picnic / Grilling

Playground

BE
BERGGASTHAUS OBERSTOCKENALP

The Two Lake Loop

START
Chrindi
(lift station)

FINISH
Chrindi
(lift station)

🏠	⊢	↗	↘	⋏	🎚
1776 m	6.3 km	366 m	367 m	1777 m	T2

⊢ 4.3 km	🕐 2:10 h		⊢ 2 km	🕐 1:30 h
Day 1			**Day 2**	
↗ 347 m	↘ 176 m		↗ 19 m	↘ 191 m

Berggasthaus
Oberstockenalp

Overview

Located in the Simmen Valley, this small area is tranquil. The hike is the perfect way to spend a weekend without having to put forth too much effort. Once off the lift at Chrindi, make your way down to Hinderstockesee. Plan to slowly ease into the day, allowing the views to captivate you. Find a picnic bench, pick-up a bag of game pieces located in the hut nearby and enjoy a board game with the entire family. Move to the playground or the lake for additional pleasure while lunch cooks over the grill. When the lake grows tiresome (we know that isn't really possible) start your hike up to the mountain house. Weaving up the mountain and through forests, know that the ascent is short. Drop off your bags and then continue on to Oberstockesee before dinner.

Directions

Day 1

Exit the Chrindi lift station, on your right as you walk away from the gondola. The trail begins down the mountain road heading toward the lake, Hinderstockesee. There is a playground and large rocking horse behind the lift station, and another play area approximately 300 m down the road on the edge of the lake. The trail will continue around the lake, counter clockwise along the right side. At the back of the lake, the trail will ascend past a farm, turn right, and begin to zig-zag up the mountain. Once the switchbacks stop, turn right at the fork, following signs for Oberstockenalp. The trail begins to level out and emerges from the forest. Berggasthaus Oberstockenalp will be visible. Drop off your bags and enjoy a pleasant walk around Oberstockesee. Follow the signs past the mountain house, which will lead down toward the lake that is visible beyond the trees. This is an easy loop, following signs back to Oberstockenalp.

Day 2

To return to Chrindi, follow the directions in reverse toward Hinderstockesee and Chrindi.

Trail Markers

Day 1

Chrindi >> Hinterstockenalp >> Oberstockenalp

Day 2

Oberstockenalp >> Hinterstockenalp >> Chrindi

Accommodation Overview

Berggasthaus Oberstockenalp is a modest house offering refuge for the evening. The staff is welcoming and the house offers basic dormitories in the eaves of the attic and one shared communal bathroom. The meals are wholesome and the dining room atmosphere is lively. For those looking for a special experience, consider sleeping in one of the three "Garden Igloos" in the front of the house under the stars. Make sure to reserve these novelty stays in advance. The house makes their own cheese, which is delicious. Yum!

Accommondation Details

Mountain House Oberstockenalp
3762 Erlenback i.S. / info@obertockenalp.ch / +41 33 681 14 88
www.oberstockenalp.ch / GPS: 46.68938, 7.53014

+ Private rooms and dormitory with sleep sacks required
+ One shared bathroom, no shower
+ No heat in the room
+ Electricity, but no outlets in the room
+ No Wi-Fi
+ Good cellular connectivity
+ Vegetarian meals available – order in advance
+ Cash only

Kid Approved

+ Two playgrounds are located along the route.
  One located at the Chrindi lift station and the other at Hinderstockesee.
+ Animal spotting is possible along the trail, including cows, pigs,
  salamanders, tadpoles, frogs and fish.
+ Games on the picnic tables at Hinderstockesee,
  making this a fun place to stop for a picnic.

Tip

Try the Oberstocken coffee with plum liqueur, which is a delicious and intoxicating way to end any day.

For a very cool experience, consider raclette in a cave at Stockhorn. To read more about this special event, and to view available dates visit: www.stockhorn.ch

Special Features

+ This is pleasant hike for families of all ages.
+ Two beautiful lakes to discover as you hike.
+ Fishing opportunities. Fishing licenses can be purchased at the Stockhornbahn as a combination ticket with the lift.
+ For spectacular views on a clear day, take the lift up to Stockhorn 2,190 m. Views of Lake Thun and the Jura are visible from this vantage point.
+ If you are a running enthusiast, consider entering or watching the Stockhorn Half Marathon in late July.
+ The Erlenbach im Simmental lift accepts the *Halbtax* and the Junior Card. For more information visit www.stockhorn.ch
+ Parking is available at Erlenbach.

Be Aware

+ Check lift and funicular operating times before heading out on your adventure.
+ There is a toilet at the Chrindi lift station and again at Hinderstockesee.
+ Bring house shoes for your overnight stay.
+ Pack layers for sleeping, as the house gets quite cold in the evening.
+ Use caution when hiking through cow pastures, especially when calves are present.
+ Camping is forbidden in the entire Stockhorn area.

J F M A **M J J A S O N** D

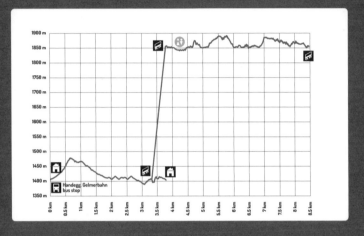

 Picnic / Grilling

Toilet

BE
HOTEL AND NATURE RESORT HANDECK

A Retreat in the Forest

6

START
Handegg, Gelmerbahn
(bus stop)

FINISH
Handegg, Gelmerbahn
(bus stop)

| 1405 m | 8.6 km | 530 m | 530 m | 1859 m | T2 |

3.9 km	1:30 h		4.7 km	2:30 h
Day 1			**Day 2**	
235 m	235 m		295 m	295 m

Hotel and Nature Resort Handeck

Overview

Nestled among trees and deep valleys, Handeck Hotel and Nature Resort is a genuine oasis for the entire family. Use this family-friendly resort as a gateway to explore Grimsel and the surrounding areas. Abundant with nature, including, glaciers, hiking trails, the alp climbing garden, lakes, and the resort is a place to indulge. This area is worthy of at least two nights to truly unwind.

As you settle into the resort, determine as a family how you would like to spend your day. Would you like to linger in the outdoor heated pool? Relax in a lounge chair as the children play at the playground? Or elect for a wild adventure by taking the hair raising, 106% gradient Gelmerbahn Funicular up to Gelmersee? Once at the impressive lake, consider walking around its shores to take in the turquoise waters. Get ready for one memorable ride.

Another excursion that provides an educational experience for the entire family is the underground tour of the KWO Power Plant. Book your tickets in advance to learn how the dam harnesses energy. The tour will allow you to understand the impressive history, all the while exploring the crystal cave located deep within the mountain. This experience will leave a lasting impression on your children, but review the website for age appropriateness before embarking on this journey.

To witness a close encounter with a glacier, visit the Rhone Glacier by the Hotel Belvédère. This glacier provides a stark visual of how global warming is impacting the glaciers in Switzerland. Though quite sad and alarming, the opportunity to educate ourselves and our children is essential.

Don't forget to participate in the thrilling drive on the Grimsel Pass, which is exciting and scenic, especially in good weather. Another added bonus of staying at the Hotel and Nature Resort Handeck is that they offer their guests free use of their electric car. Check with the front desk about booking the car for all of your local excursions.

Once your time has come to an end, you will feel refreshed and rejuvenated, just in time for your next hiking adventure!

Directions

Hike 1 — The Crystal Trail Loop

The trail begins at the Alpkäserei Handegg and can be completed in either direction by heading toward the hanging bridge or uphill behind the *Käserei*. When heading past the *Käserei*, the trail will run along the edge of a field before zig-zagging uphill and through the forest. After approximately 800 m, look for a spur on your right toward a small crystal cave. The trail continues and will come to a grilling/picnic area after another 600 m. The trail will continue toward the main road. Use caution when crossing the road, as the cars travel quickly. After the road, you will pass a farmhouse. Head down toward the river (Aare). Caution! The river may be impassable in the rain. Just past the river, the trail connects with a road, leading to the Gelmerbahn funicular station and the hanging bridge. Cross the bridge and complete the loop arriving at the *Käserei*.

Hike 2 — The Gelmersee Loop

This hiking loop requires a reservation on the Gelmerbahn funicular, so plan in advance. Once off the funicular, walk in the direction of the lake. Veering right, the trail will lead past a building with a toilet, and then turn left to cross over the dam. Once across the dam, the trail will turn left again, on a narrow path between the lake and a rock face. There is a waterfall in this area, which may make the trail impassable during rain. The trail will climb uphill slightly and then descend again toward the back of the lake. There is a second, even narrower section at the back of the lake, so use caution. The trail will ascend again, turn left, and will head back along the opposite side of the lake toward the funicular station.

Trail Markers

Are not applicable for these hikes.

Accommodation Overview

Hotel and Nature Resort Handeck has it all. Crisp linens, private bathrooms, friendly staff and family activities in the area. Enjoy a true gem in the mountains! Linger over a decadent meal in the gorgeous dining room and allow the children ample time to explore. Truly, you won't want to leave. We know because we didn't!

Acommondation Details

Hotel and Nature Resort Handeck
3864 Guttannen / hotels@grimselwelt.ch / +41 33 982 36 11
www.grimselwelt.ch / GPS: 46.61203, 8.30789

+ Family rooms and double rooms available
+ All linens, towels and toiletries are provided by the hotel.
+ Private bathrooms
+ Heat in the rooms
+ Electricity and outlets in the rooms
+ Free Wi-Fi
+ Good cellular connectivity
+ Vegetarian options available, request at the time of booking
+ Cash and credit cards accepted

Kid Approved

+ The resident pigs, which are smelly, but quite cute!
+ The playground at the resort, including the trampoline.
+ The Gelmerbahn Funicular, which to a child feels a bit like a rollercoaster.
+ The crystal trail in close proximity to the hotel.
+ The Rhone Glacier is worth a visit to educate your children about the impacts of global warming

Tip

For families with a car, consider a day trip to Hasliberg to complete one or both of the Muggestutz Dwarf Trails as outlined in our first book. These charming trails are ideal for children ages four through ten.

Special Features

+ The family friendliness of the hotel is outstanding.
+ The gourmet menu is a culinary delight each evening.
+ The heated, outdoor swimming pool, which provides
  the perfect activity in rainy weather.
+ The onsite spa for adults because sometimes we too, need to chill out.
+ The workout room, in the event you haven't hiked enough.
+ There is an onsite *Alpkäserei*.
+ The nature in the surrounding area is rich with trees
  and impressive mountains.
+ The endless activities that are available in the immediate area.

Be Aware

+ Reserve the hotel far in advance as it books up quickly.
+ You may never want to leave this incredible resort.
  Prepare for melancholy upon departure.
+ You might just become slightly spoiled.
+ Reserve the Gelmerbahn Funicular and KWO tour in advance
  of your trip. Ticket purchases the day of can be problematic as
  there are limited spaces and running times. Allow for approximately
  3–3.5 hours to hike around the lake. For more details visit:
  www.grimselwelt.ch

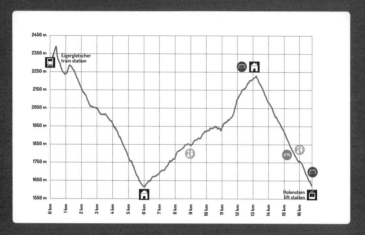

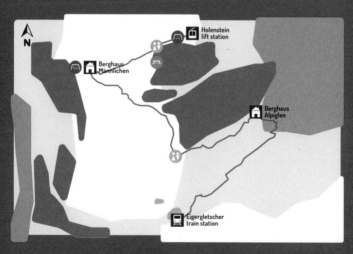

 Picnic / Grilling

Playground

Toilet

The Eiger Tour

START
Eigergletscher
(train station)

FINISH
Holenstein
(lift station)

1616 m 2225 m	16.4 km	773 m	1481 m	2320 m	T2

	Day 1		Day 2		Day 3
5.7 km	3:30 h	7 km	3:15 h	3.7 km	1:50 h
91 m	786 m	677 m	86 m	5 m	609 m

Berghaus Alpiglen

Berghaus Männlichen

Overview

The Eiger trail is a complete and total wonder. Brace yourself for breathtaking views throughout this epic hike. Despite the posted time, plan to double the time based on the number of stops you will be making to absorb the beauty of this route. In addition, your neck may hurt from constantly looking at the face of the Eiger as you witness its ever-changing landscape. As you make your way to Alpiglen, enjoy the waterfalls, alpine flowers and the mountains in the distance.

The next morning, you will make your way to Männlichen through meandering paths and forests. The walk is relatively easy with a few uphill sections. Once at Männlichen, if the weather permits, plan on allotting hours of playtime at the expansive and very impressive playground adjacent to the *Berghaus*.

After a restful evening, opt to take the theme trail "Lieselotte" (pick-up an informational brochure at the lift station), which encourages the children to get up close and personal to the life of a cow. With the story of Lieselotte, who is a cow that comes from a tiny village in Germany, children will have the opportunity to ring cow bells, and learn how to milk. Children will have fun as they climb structures and stamp their cards as they pass through this 3.7 km trail. This is the perfect way to make your way down the mountain and finally to Holenstein before being swept down the mountain to Grindelwald. This tour will end with broad smiles on the faces of your children.

Directions

Day 1

Exit the Eigergletscher station following signs toward Eiger Trail Alpiglen. The trail will begin to descend and then will rise just below the Rotstock summit, approximately at the 1.2 km mark. There is a trail sign which points out the Eiger north face climbing routes. At this point look up to the right; look for climbers scaling a series of ladders between the Rotstock peak and the Eiger north face. If you look left, can you find the Eiger Station? There is an emergency access from the Jungfraubahn to the middle of the north face below the summit. Hint: It appears as a series of light rectangles in a patch of gray rock. The trail continues descending until a waterfall appears at about the 4.2 km. At this point, the trail will descend steeper toward Alpiglen, which will appear just over a kilometer away.

Day 2

From Alpiglen, follow signs toward Männlichen, heading uphill. Within one kilometer, you will cross the cogwheel railway; use caution. The trail will continue to parallel the railway and will be visible above on the left. The trail continues and will veer right at a cluster of lift stations at Arvengarten, where there is a toilet. The trail continues past a few farm houses and uphill. Keep left toward Männlichen. The trail continues above the treeline and under several chairlift cables (not running in summer) until the ridge appears just before Männlichen. The *Berghotel* is just behind the Männlichen lift station.

Day 3

The trail starts just in front of the *Berghotel*. Proceed downhill toward Holenstein/ Grindelwald, parallel to several chair lifts. This section is themed as the "Lieselotte" trail with 13 stations. After approximately 2 km, there is a grilling/picnic area on the right near a stream. Just below this area is a farm house that sells cheese. There is a toilet just past the farmhouse at the lift station Hinter der Egg. The trail continues down to lift station Holenstein where there is a playground and another picnic area. You can take the lift at Holenstein to return to Grindelwald.

Trail Markers

Day 1
Eigergletscher » Alpiglen

Day 2
Alpiglen » Bustiglen » Männlichen

Day 3
Männlichen » Läger » Holenstein

Accommodation Overview
for Berghaus Alpiglen

Apligen is a sweet little mountain house surrounded by picturesque views and tiny chalets. Double rooms are available in the main house and the dormitories are located in a separate building. The rooms are tidy and the dining area is welcoming. The meals offered are delicious and served with care. A walk around the area at night is the perfect way to end your first day.

Alpiglen Details

Berghaus Alpiglen
3818 Grindelwald / info@alpiglen.ch / +41 33 853 11 30
www.alpiglen.ch / GPS: 46.60032, 8.00416

+ Sleeping sacks required in the dormitories
+ Shared bathrooms with showers in the main building
+ Towels recommended for the dormitory, though available for rent.
  Towels are provided in the private rooms.
+ Heat in the rooms
+ Electricity and outlets in the room
+ No Wi-Fi
+ Good cellular connectivity
+ À la carte menu – vegetarian options available on the menu
+ Cash and credit cards accepted

Accommodation Overview for Berghaus Männlichen

The panoramic views from the mountain house at Männlichen are stunning. Männlichen is a huge hit with the children because of their incredibly constructed play area, which boasts a massive wooden cow. The cow is so beautifully crafted that it resembles a piece of fine art.

The area is home to multiple theme trails, including the Royal Walk, which will take you up to the Männlichen summit in just 1 km. This easy, though uphill route, can be completed from the mountain house. Enjoy the comforts of the house.

Männlichen Details

Berghaus Männlichen

3818 Grindelwald / info@berghaus-maennlichen.ch / +41 33 853 10 68
www.berghaus-maennlichen.ch / GPS: 46.61147, 7.94221

+ Family rooms available, request at your time of booking
+ Private bathrooms with shower
+ Heat in the room
+ Electricity and outlets in the room
+ Free Wi-Fi
+ Good cellular connectivity
+ Vegetarian options available
+ Cash and credit cards accepted

Kid Approved

+ Prepare yourself; your children might even be awe-struck by the views on this one!
+ If you want to see if there are climbers on the Eiger, don't forget your binoculars.
+ The playground at Alpiglen is modest, but fun.
+ The totally awesome playground at Berghaus Männlichen is mind blowing.
+ The "Lieselotte" theme trail from Männlichen to Holenstein
  is a fun way to end this tour.

Tip

This area can be particularly crowded, especially at the Kleine Scheidegg train station. Plan for crowds, keep your children close and be patient. Once you are on the trail, the crowds should lessen. You can hike from Klein Scheidegg; this will add approximately 2.3 km to day 1.

Special Features

+ The views on the first leg of this hike are epic!
+ The child-centric aspects of this tour.
+ UNESCO World Heritage Site – Swiss Alps Jungfrau – Aletsch
+ The Eiger Trail is one of the top 12 most beautiful trails in Switzerland.
+ The trail overlaps part of the St. Petronell path, which provided access between Bern and Valais between the 12th and 16th centuries.
+ Look for the Swiss-O-Finder posts and tags along the way, this is part of an orienteering/running trail, for more information visit at www.swiss-o-finder.ch
+ The trail also overlaps the Via Alpina, Green Route, for more information visit: www.via-alpina.org
+ The lifts in the area accept *Halbtax* and Junior Cards, for more information visit: www.jungfrau.ch

Be Aware

+ Rock falls are possible on the Eiger North Face Trail. Use caution when hiking this trail.
+ Only one toilet at Arvengarten on the second day. No water filling stations along the trails.
+ Hiking poles are recommended for this route.
+ Pack layers of clothing for additional warmth on this route.
+ This tour is not recommended in poor or winter weather.
+ Harnesses may be helpful for children on the Eiger North Face Trail.
+ The Männlichen summer season is from early June through the end of October. The winter season is from the beginning of December through the middle of April.
+ The new V-Bahn may alter the accuracy of the listed access points.
+ You can print out the PDF for the "Lieselotte" theme trail before you go. For more information visit www.maennlichen.ch (German only)

J F M A M J J A S O **N** D

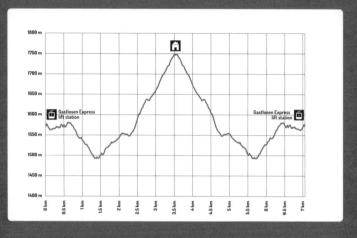

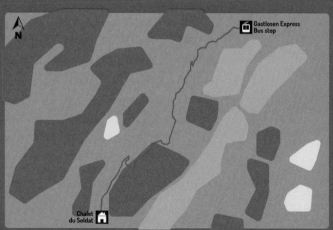

Snowshoeing Trek

START
Jaun, Kappelboden
(bus stop)

FINISH
Jaun, Kappelboden
(bus stop)

1752 m	7 km	402 m	402 m	1752 m	T2

3.5 km	3:20 h		3.5 km	2:10 h
Day 1			**Day 2**	
287 m	115 m		115 m	287 m

Chalet
du Soldat

Overview

Dust off those snowshoes and get ready for a gorgeous winter excursion. During the snow season, this trek provides the opportunity to step outside into a winter wonderland and seek shelter for the night in a perfectly positioned chalet.

Don't forget to take in the setting sun over the Gastlosen range positioned perfectly in front of the chalet. The Gastlosen range, extends from Jaun to Rougemont and lights up the sky. Wrap yourselves up in wooly sweaters, enjoy the warmth of the fire in the main dining hall and welcome the evening with a good meal and quality family time. The next morning, wake early to witness the sunrise before you begin your return journey back through open trails, woods and ultimately down the mountain.

Directions

Day 1
From the Jaun, Kappelboden bus stop, follow signs toward Schattenhalb. The tickets for the Gastlosen Express can be purchased at the kiosk in the parking area. Take the lift up; at the top is Musersbergli. Follow signs toward Soldatenhaus. The trail in winter is easy to follow and is on a well-marked, pink, snowshoe route. The trail will take you in and out of the forest. The last climb leads you out of the forest from Ober Sattel. The chalet is not visible until the last 25 m as you crest the hill. Enjoy the view!

Day 2
The return can be made by following the directions in reverse.

Trail Markers

Day 1
Kappelboden Jaun ≫ Gastlosen Lift ≫ Musersbergli ≫ Soldatenhaus

Day 2
Soldatenhaus ≫ Musersbergli ≫ Gastlosen Lift ≫ Kappelboden Juan

Accommodation Overview

The chalet is located in a lovely setting and invites hikers/snowshoers into its cozy dining hall to enjoy a meal around the warmth of the wood burning stove. The chalet offers functional accommodations in dormitory rooms.

This hut has a fascinating history inspired by Paul Wolf, who was in command of the mountain hunters in the 16th battalion in 1943. Wolf realized mountain troops needed a sufficient place for alpine training both during the winter and summer months. His lofty idea of building such a location was born and that vision helped create the modern-day Chalet du Soldat. After tremendous work, planning, and support from other captains, architects and engineers, the construction of the training facility was finally realized in 1945.

Acommondation Details

Chalet du Soldat
1656 Jaun / info@chaletdusoldat.ch / +41 26 929 82 35 / +41 79 247 63 32
www.chaletdusoldat.ch / GPS: 46.57646, 7.2635

+ Dormitories only, sleeping sacks required
  Bring warm sleep sacks during the winter months
+ Shared bathrooms, no showers
+ No drinking water; however, water is available for purchase
+ Electricity and outlets in the room
+ Free Wi-Fi
+ Moderate cellular connectivity
+ À la carte menu – vegetarian options available
+ Cash and credit card accepted

Kid Approved

+ The opportunity to sled and snowshoe in winter.
+ Chamois spotting, so don't forget your binoculars.
+ The ability to track animal footprints in the snow.

Tips

Noah
Pack warm clothes if you stay the night in the chalet during the winter months.

Parents
Start this snowshoeing tour early during the winter months. With the lack of light hours, you want to have plenty of time to arrive at the chalet before dark.

Special Features

+ This route is void of crowds.
+ This trek offers a nice mix of uphill and downhill with the snowshoes.
+ Picturesque views throughout.
+ This route can be completed in the summer months as well.
+ It is possible to sled down to Jaun on the return from the hut.
  Sleds may be available from Jaun Bergbahn.

Be Aware

+ The sunsets are early in the winter months, so plan accordingly.
+ There are no toilets on the route.
+ No drinking water available on the route.
+ Bring poles when snowshoeing.
+ In winter, pack warm clothes and layers for the chalet.
  The chalet is not particularly warm, but is heated by
  a wood burning stove in the main dining area only.
+ Confirm the chalet is open and reservations have been confirmed
  prior to your arrival.
+ The lift from Jaun does not accept the *Halbtax* or Junior cards, but it
  does offer free parking, for more information visit:
  www.jaun-bergbahnen.ch

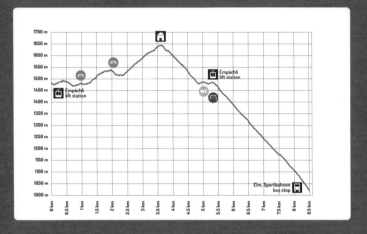

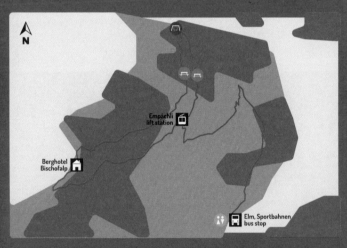

Picnic / Grilling

Playground

Toilet

GL
BERGHOTEL BISCHOFALP

A Weekend of Play

9

START
Empächli
(lift station)

FINISH
Elm, Sportbahnen
(bus stop)

| 1650 m | 8.6 km | 332 m | 775 m | 1650 m | T1 |

3.5 km	2:30 h	5.1 km	2:25 h
Day 1		**Day 2**	
244 m	61 m	88 m	714 m

Berghotel
Bischofalp

Overview

This easy and delightful hike engages the children from the moment they step off the gondola at Ämpächli (Empächli). With trampolines and Elmar's Goldmine (children can pick-up pans to mine for gold at the nearby restaurant), your children will want to spend hours at this play area. With a tree house, slide, geometric figure for climbing and a pretty awesome swing, it will be hard to tear the children away from the play area to start the hike. Don't worry: the Giant Forest ("Riesenwald") theme trail is full of activities for children of all ages, so the fun won't stop at the playground. With 17 stations along the theme trail and plenty of opportunities to grill, take your time and enjoy this easy-going 2.5 km path. After a day of recreation and exploration, make your way to the Berghotel for a relaxing evening.

Directions

Day 1

Exit the Empächli lift station and turn right. Ahead, slightly down the hill, you will see a large play area next to Restaurant Ämpächli. Behind the restaurant is the start of the "Riesenwald" theme trail. Follow the signs through the field and into the forest. There are several stations along the way and roughly 1 km into the trail, it will switchback; at this location there is a large grill area with a play area. Continuing on and another 200 m, there is a large zip-line. There are several grill areas before the trail emerges from the forest, and arrives at the Älpli Restaurant. Continue past the restaurant following signs for Bischofalp, which is just past a small chairlift.

Day 2

The next day, hike in the direction of Ämpächli Oberstaffel. This will take you toward Hengstboden, a historic and picturesque cluster of farmhouses. The trail will switchback here and head back to the Empächli lift station where you can choose to play, take the lift down, take *Trotti* bikes, or hike down. To hike down, follow the signs toward Elm, which will lead downhill from the lift. Caution! Do not follow the Mountain/*Trotti* bikes trail if hiking. The trail will continue along a road, until the road switches back, but the trail heads straight off the road. The trail continues downhill on and off mountain roads until it arrives at lift station at the bottom (use caution with cars and *Trotti* bikes!). The Elm, Sportbahn bus station is in front of the lift station on the main road.

Trail Markers

Day 1

Ämpächli ≫ Chuenz ≫ Rietmatt (Berghotel Bischofalp)

Day 2

Rietmatt (Berghotel Bischofalp) ≫ Hengstboden ≫ Unter Empächli ≫ Ämpächli ≫ Gerstboden ≫ Schäboden ≫ Talstastion

Accommodation Overview

Bischofalp is a truly luxurious accommodation with modern charm. With beautifully appointed family rooms, private bathrooms, and some rooms with a loft area for the children to sleep, you might wish to linger a little while longer and soak in this lovely hotel. The views are not too bad either!

Accommondation Details

Bischofalp Berghotel

8767 Elm / restaurant@bischofalp.ch / +41 55 642 15 25
www.bischofalp.ch / GPS: 46.9184, 9.14224

+ Private rooms with sheets, duvets and towels
+ Private bathroom located in the room
+ Heat in the room
+ Electricity and outlets in the room
+ Free Wi-Fi
+ Good cellular connectivity
+ Vegetarian options available, request at the time of booking
+ Cash and credit cards accepted

Kid Approved

+ The playground at Ämpächli (Empächli) is awesome.
+ Mining for gold is pretty cool.
+ The "Riesenwald" theme trail is the perfect way to spend the afternoon.
+ The opportunity to feed goats (yes, this is permissible)
  under the lift station at Ämpächli.
+ Crystals for sale on the theme trail, and cheese.

Tip

There is a water fountain at station 10 along the "Riesenwald" theme trail; however, it is not drinking water. Please do not drink the water from this fountain; pack plenty of water.

Special Features

+ This is a family fun destination.
+ Lush, green, mountainous landscapes are visible throughout.
+ Plenty of additional hiking/snowshoeing trails in the area.
  This is also a great winter destination.
+ UNESCO World Heritage Site – Swiss Tectonic Arena Sardona.
+ Martin's Hole, which is a literal hole in the mountain range across
  from Elm that twice per year the sun shines directly through.
  The sun, on those two special days, will shine straight
  onto the small church of Elm.
+ For additional pleasure, consider a visit to the Läderach chocolate
  factory located just 20 km by car or 45 minutes by train
  in the town of Ennenda. For more information visit
  houseofladerach.com
+ Did you know there is a slate mine in the area? Learn about mining
  slate (tour a slate mine in the neighbouring town of Matt) and its uses,
  or make your own chalkboard (in the town of Elm).
  For more information visit www.landesplattenberg.ch
+ The Sportbahn Elm does not accept the *Halbtax* nor the Junior Card.
  For more information visit www.sportbahnenelm.ch

Be Aware

+ Always check lift-operating times.
+ Pack layers for warmth.
+ Toilets are located at the Sportbahnen Elm lift station, the restaurant
  at Ämpächli (Empächli) and there is one along the Riesenwald theme
  trail (station 10).
+ Be careful with the *Trotti* bikes that share the trail with the hikers,
  should you elect to hike from Ämpächli (Empächli) down to Elm.

J F M A M J J A S O N D

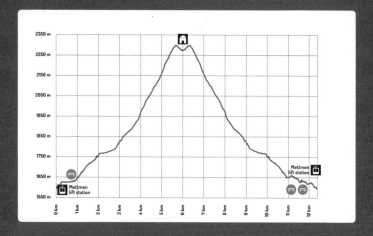

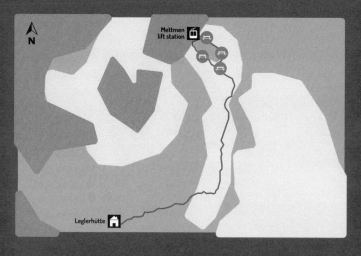

Picnic / Grilling

Pure Nature in the Mountains

START
Mettmen
(lift station)

FINISH
Mettmen
(lift station)

| 2273 m | 11.8 km | 774 m | 774 m | 2294 m | T2 |

5.9 km	3:30 h	5.9 km	3 h
Day 1		**Day 2**	
716 m	58 m	58 m	716 m

Leglerhütte
SAC

Overview

Some regions will forever etch themselves into your being and Glarnerland does just that. With stunning views throughout and pure nature, take the time to breathe in this area. Your climb to the top of Leglerhütte will be marked with lakes, look out points and dramatic mountain views. Despite having to work to reach the hut, allow the views to provide the motivation to carry you through this hike.

Once you reach the top, you will find yourself breathless from the climb and from the 360° views. Now that you have arrived, sit back and enjoy a beer or homemade cake, as the children splash around in the small lake onsite. Get comfortable and ready for a night of stunning sunsets and a room that provides the most majestic view as the sun sinks low and kisses the horizon. Though we are not supposed to have favorites, Leglerhütte is extraordinary and the memories from that weekend will surely linger.

Directions

Day 1

Exit the Mettmen lift station and follow the path toward Berggasthaus Mettmenalp. The trail signs next to the mountain house will direct you toward Stausee Garichti (lake) and *Weitere Wegweiser* (more trail signs). At the next signpost you will see signs for Leglerhütte SAC along with additional signs about the wildlife in the area. Continue along the edge of the lake. At the back of the lake, the trail will ascend for about 1 km until a large wooden lookout tower is visible. The trail levels off until a farmhouse with the Kärpfbrücke (Chärpfbrugg) behind it. Optional: you can enter the cave, keeping left at this entrance, but use caution as it is wet, narrow and dark. The trail continues around the natural bridge and over the top of it. Use caution at the top as the trail is next to the mouth of the cave, which is a drop off. Shortly after the natural bridge, the trail splits; continue straight. Just under a kilometer later, the trail will split again; take the right trail continuing toward Leglerhütte SAC. The trail will begin to climb, and zig-zag through fields and rocks. Take your time, this is the last two kilometers and the last kilometer meanders through and over rocky terrain. This part of the trail is partially on the north side of the mountain ridge, Unter Chärpf, so there may be snow into July. Leglerhütte is just over a rise, and is visible during the last 350 m.

Day 2

Follow the directions in reverse for the return.

Trail Markers

Day 1

Mettmen ❯❯ Mettmen Staumauer ❯❯ Nideren Oberstafel ❯❯ Chärpfbrugg ❯❯ Untere Hübschböden ❯❯ Hübschbodensee ❯❯ Leglerhütte SAC

Day 2

Leglerhütte SAC ❯❯ Hübschbodensee ❯❯ Untere Hübschböden ❯❯ Chärpfbrugg ❯❯ Nideren Oberstafel ❯❯ Mettmen Staumauer ❯❯ Mettmen

Accommodation Overview

Leglerhütte is positioned in a captivating location, which might just take your breath away at first sight. The hut is clean and dining room is welcoming. The small dormitory rooms offer bunk beds and a picture window. Don't spend too much time inside as you might miss the opportunity to catch a stunning sunset. Your children will enjoy splashing in the small pond. Dinner is a communal event, served with care.

Acommondation Details

Leglerhütte SAC
8750 Glarus / +41 55 640 81 77 / +41 78 684 75 32
leglerhuette.ch / GPS: 46.9274, 9.08023

+ Private, modest dormitories. Sleep sacks and pillowcases required
+ Shared bathrooms without shower
+ No heat in the rooms
+ Electricity, but no outlets in the room
+ No Wi-Fi
+ Good cellular connectivity
+ Fixed menu. Vegetarian options – book in advance
+ Cash only accepted

Kid Approved

+ There is a lake (Stausee Garichti) at the start of the hike and a pond at Leglerhütte where frogs, newts and tadpoles might just be hiding. Look carefully!
+ Early in the morning during our descent, we spotted lots of frogs on the trail. Watch where you step and have fun counting the number of frogs you discover on the way down the mountain!

Tip

Be patient during this hike. Take lots of breaks and allow sufficient time to reach the hut. Bring your children's favorite snacks with you, pack plenty of water and games (refer to chapter four) to provide entertainment along the way. You will all work to get up the mountain, but we promise you won't be disappointed upon your arrival.

On our descent, the clouds and fog quickly moved in, making visibility poor. Use caution when descending and use your map/tracking device to return to your destination point if necessary.

Special Features

+ This hike and the hut location provide 360° views.
+ This area is very special and quite rich with wildlife.
  We were able to spot chamois, fox, frogs, tadpoles, newts,
  golden eagles, and salamanders.
+ There are abundant waterfalls and lakes throughout.
+ This area is part of the Freiberg Kärpf and is the oldest wildlife reserve
  in Europe – at over 450 years old!
+ The hut does not have Wi-Fi. This is your chance to truly disconnect.
  Yippee!
+ UNSESCO World Heritage Site – Swiss Tectonic Arena Sardona

Be Aware

+ The hike to the hut is a long and a steady climb.
  Get an early start on this one.
+ There are no water filling stations or toilets along the route. Use the
  toilet at the lift station before starting out.
+ The terrain is very rocky throughout.
+ There may be snow and snowfields in the summer months that must
  be crossed. Use caution and help each other across such areas.
+ Pack warm clothing, as the hut does not have heat. Warm sleeping
  sacks are recommended.
+ Due to the location of the hut, the weather changes quickly.
  Be prepared.
+ There are several steep drop-offs around the hut. Watch children
  carefully in these areas.

| J | F | M | A | M | J | J | A | S | O | N | D |

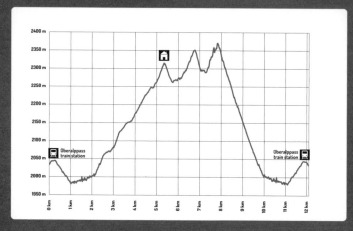

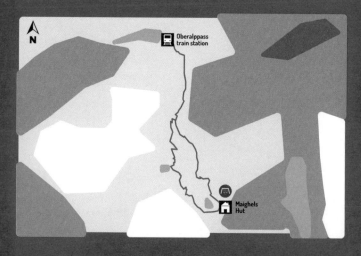

Playground

GR
MAIGHELSHÜTTE SAC

Rhine Source Loop

11

START
Oberalppass
(train station)

FINISH
Oberalppass
(train station)

| 🏠 2310 m | ↔ 11.6 km | ↗ 620 m | ↘ 620 m | ⋀ 2362 m | ⇅ T2 |

↔ 5.1 km	⏱ 2:30 h	↔ 6.5 km	⏱ 3:15 h
Day 1		**Day 2**	
↗ 369 m	↘ 79 m	↗ 251 m	↘ 541 m

Maighelshütte SAC

Overview

Upon your arrival at Oberalp Pass, the views across Oberalp Lake are captivating, with rugged alpine peaks jutting out in the distance. The busy pass is soon exchanged for calming nature as you trek into the valley along the trail. The Maighels hut is tucked away in an isolated alpine valley and shares this location with the source of the Rhine River. The trail takes you into the nature reserve of Stavel da Maighels. As you walk through an alpine pasture take the time to look back where you came from, as the landscape ahead is contrasted by the expansive views back toward the pass. As you approach the Maighels hut, the view up the Maighels Valley is equally stunning with glaciers in the distance.

Directions

Day 1
From the Oberalppass train station, walk up the hill toward Restaurant Piz Calmot, past the restaurant, and walk through the parking lot. You will see a lighthouse next to an information kiosk. Continue past the kiosk; the trail will parallel the main road through a grass area for about one kilometer. The trail will meander along and through pastures. At about the 4 km point, just after the switch-back in the road, there is an outcropping of rock which is a good site for rock climbing. The hut is one kilometer farther.

Day 2
Walk down the road from the hut, crossing to the other side of the valley following signs toward Lai da Tuma. This trail is a direct route zig-zagging up and down (and back up again) to the lake. This is a tranquil lake, and a good spot for a picnic. The trail will then descend with switchbacks until reconnecting with the trail from the day before. Turn left and follow signs back to Oberalp Pass.

Trail Markers

Day 1
Oberalppass >> Maighelshütte SAC (Cna. da Maighels CAS)

Day 2
Maighelshütte SAC (Cna. da Maighels CAS) >> Lai da Tuma >> Oberalppass

Accommodation Overview

Positioned on the southwesterly face of Piz Cavradi, the hut is hidden in a valley, offering peace and quiet from Oberalp Pass. The hut provides a family-friendly atmosphere, inviting visitors to slow down, take pleasure in the views, or have a drink while the children play. The sleeping arrangements are various dormitory rooms. Water and *Marschtee* (tea brewed by the hut) are available upon request.

Acommodation Details

Maighelshütte SAC
7189 Tujetsch / info@maighelshuette.ch / +41 81 949 15 51
www.maighelshuette.ch / GPS: 46.62528, 8.69006

+ Dormitories only, sleep sack required
+ Shared bathrooms and pay for showers
+ Heat in the room
+ Electricity, but no outlets in the room
+ No Wi-Fi
+ Weak cellular connectivity
+ Fixed menu. Vegetarian options available, request at the time of booking
+ Cash and credit cards accepted

Kid Approved

+ Swings and a slack-line are at the hut, as is a climbing garden on the way.

Tip

For a longer T3 adventure, this can be extended into a tour on the second day (+8.6 km). Cross Passo Bornengo (2,631 m) with a second overnight at Capanna Cadlimo CAS (2,570 m) and on the third day (+8.6 km) hike down, past lake Ritom (Lago Ritom) to the funicular station Piora. If you choose this tour, start our mapped route in reverse so you can stop at the Lai da Tuma, the source of the Rhine.

Special Features

+ This route provides expansive alpine views high above the trees.
+ Seeing the source of one of the major rivers in Europe is impressive!
+ This route overlaps part of the 4 Source River trail, an 85 km long loop through this alpine region visiting the sources of the Rhine, Reuss, Rhone, and Ticino rivers, more information can be found at: www.vier-quellen-weg.ch

Be Aware

+ Camona da Maighels CAS and Maighelshütte SAC are synonymous.
+ At higher elevations, it is important to drink plenty of water.
+ Bring plenty of snacks and water for this route.
+ No toilets along the route; plan accordingly.
+ Poles may be helpful for this hike.

J F M A M J J A S O N D

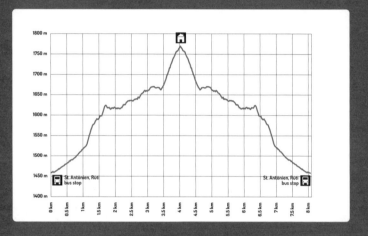

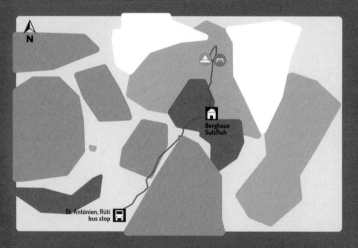

Picnic / Grilling

Boat rental

GR
BERGHAUS SULZFLUH
Step Back
in Time

START
St. Antönien, Rüti
(bus stop)

| 1772 m | 8.2 km | 381 m | 381 m | 1880 m | T2 |

4.1 km	2 h	
Day 1		
337 m	44 m	

4.1 km	1:30 h	
Day 2		
44 m	337 m	

Berghaus
Sulzfluh

Overview

This is a marvelous hike offering up big views with a peaceful overnight stay at the historic Berghaus Sulzfluh. The hike meanders along a river, through a forest, over rocky sections, and ultimately up to the *Berghaus*. This route seems to have it all, making it ideal for the seasoned traveler. For additional pleasure, extend your hike on to the gorgeous lake (Partnunsee), which is tucked away from view. This idyllic spot is perfect for a slow walk and with the small climbing garden, your children may want to attempt bouldering. Please know that hiking to the lake will add approximately three extra kilometers to the total distance.

Once at the *Berghaus*, enjoy this historic house dating back to 1875. Relax in the nostalgic dining room where candlelight creates a warm glow, the floorboards creak with every move you make, and history is bound tightly into the wooden walls. At dinner, take pleasure in eating the three-course meal, and if the weather is cold, unwind by the fire. Bring a game to play, or a book to read before retreating to your room for a peaceful slumber.

Directions

Day 1
From the bus stop St. Antönien, Rüti (Parking area P3), turn left out of the parking lot and again left across the bridge. Follow the road (Büel) in the direction of Partnun/Sulzfluh and past Parking areas P4 and P5. You will reach a cluster of old farm houses; the trail sign will point up the field and into the forest. The trail will continue in and out of the forest until Carschina Untersäss. You will see the road below, which is the last parking area (P6). The trail will continue to weave through fields with flowers and climb up to Partnunstaffel just next to Berghaus Sulzfluh.

Day 2
Follow the directions in reverse for the return.

Trail Markers

Day 1
St. Antonien, Rüti ≫ Carschina Untersäss ≫ Partnunstafel (Berghaus Sulzfluh)

Day 2
Partnunstafel (Berghaus Sulzfluh) ≫ Carschina Untersäss ≫ St. Antonien, Rüti

Accommodation Overview

Sulzfluh is so rich with charm you will feel immediately welcome upon your arrival. It's safe to say we adore nostalgic inns with long histories and candlelit rooms. Though there has been a modern addition added on to the house, we recommend staying in the older section to experience the true appeal of the *Berghaus*.

Acommodation Details

Berghaus Sulzfluh
7246 St. Antönien / info@sulzfluh.ch / +41 81 332 12 13
www.sulzfluh.ch / GPS: 46.99503, 9.85893

+ Modern and nostalgic rooms available and dormitory
+ Shared bathrooms with shower
+ No electricity or outlets in the nostalgic rooms
+ No Wi-Fi
+ Good cellular connectivity
+ Fixed meal – vegetarian options available, but book in advance
+ Cash and credit cards accepted

Kid Approved

+ Partnunsee is a great place for the children to get their feet wet, search for frogs, tadpoles and fish. For more adventurous families, there is even a small climbing garden.

Tip

If your intent is to hike to the lake, drop off your bags at the *Berghaus* first and pack a small bag of the essentials, including a layer for warmth.

Special Features

+ This stunning area is void of mass tourism ... shh!
  Places as enchanting as this are hard to find these days.
+ There is a playground "Steinbock Spielplatz" located at parking lot P2
  in the town of St. Antönien.
+ Car access is easy with multiple parking places available. Select the
  parking lot that is available and as close to the trailhead as you prefer
  knowing that P4 and P5 will shorten the total distance of the hike.
+ Amazing wild flowers decorate the landscape in the late spring.
+ *Trotti* bikes are available for rent to ride down the mountain.
+ Winter access is possible with snowshoes.

Be Aware

+ There is no water along the route.
+ Toilets are available at parking lots 2 and 3.
+ The *Berghaus* is closed on Monday and Tuesday each week.
+ Bring a fleece to the lake for additional warmth.
+ Paid parking at location P3, P4, & P5. There is a seasonal bus available
  beyond the P3 parking area.

J F M A M J J A S O N D

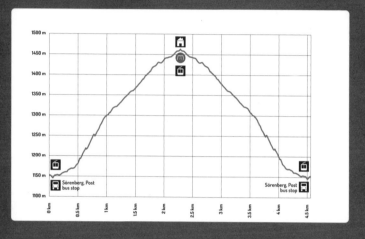

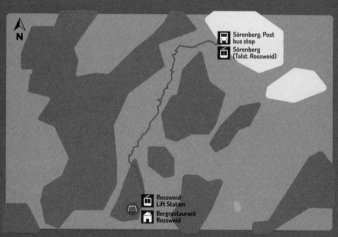

Playground

LU
BERGHOTEL ROSSWEID

Scenic Views and Family Fun

START
Sörenberg, Post
(bus stop)

FINISH
Sörenberg, Post
(bus stop)

1465 m	4.6 km	343 m	343 m	1465 m	T2

2.3 km	1 h		2.3 km	1 h
Day 1			**Day 2**	
326 m	17 m		17 m	326 m

 Berghotel
Rossweid

Overview

If you are embarking on your first hike to hut/hotel experience, this might be the ideal place to start. This laidback, uphill hike in the Upper Waldemmen Valley, offers scenic views throughout. With a mix of open trails and forests, the anticipation of what is to come should guide your steps. Once children arrive at Rossweid, the true sense of wonder begins. With an expansive playground, parents can now relax on one of the wooden benches as their children lose themselves in the small pond as they search for frogs and tadpoles. Time will slowly melt away, as your children play for hours. Berghotel Rossweid is the ideal choice for a relaxing family weekend, full of hiking trails and activities.

Directions

Day 1

From Sörenberg, Post (bus stop), cross the street and proceed over the bridge in the direction of Sörenberg Talstation. Keep right and continue up the hill. On the bend in the road, the trail veers right through a grass field before turning left and continuing uphill. The trail will continue for approximately 1.4 km; when the trail splits, take the left trail in the direction of Rossweid.

Day 2

Follow signs in reverse on the return.

Trail Markers

Day 1

Sörenberg Post (bus stop) ≫ Hinterschönisei ≫ Rossweid

Day 2

Rossweid ≫ Hinterschönisei ≫ Sörenberg Post (bus stop)

Accommodation Overview

This *Berghotel* sits in an ideal location for families of all ages. With easy-to-access trails in both winter and summer and an expansive playground, families can easily enjoy one to two nights at this family-friendly destination. The food is delicious too.

Accommodation Details

Berghotel Rossweid
6174 Sörenberg / rossweid@soerenberg.ch / +41 41 488 14 70
www.rossweid-soerenberg.ch / GPS: 46.80865, 8.02674

+ Private rooms with sheets, duvets and towels all provided
+ Private bathrooms in the rooms
+ Heat in the rooms
+ Electricity and outlets in the room
+ Free Wi-Fi
+ Moderate cellular connectivity
+ Vegetarian options available, request at the time of booking
+ Cash and credit cards accepted

Kid Approved

+ The High Rope Park ("Hochseilpark") in Sörenberg is open from May through October and suitable for older children ages 14+. For more information visit: go-in-soerenberg.ch
+ The playground at the *Berghotel* is fantastic.

Tip

During the summer months, guests at the *Berghotel* will receive the day travel card for Rossweid and the Rothorn Gondola. We highly recommend a trip up the Mt. Brienzer (2,350 m). On a clear day, allow yourself to take in the 360° views with over 693 visible peaks, including some of the greatest: Eiger, Mönch and Jungfrau.

There is also an old (1892) steam train that makes its way up the other side of the mountain to Brienzer Rothorn. Though not covered by the day travel card, this could very well be another trip that provides the entire family a memorable experience.

Special Features

+ The "Mooraculum Sörenberg Entelbuch" theme trail starts directly at the hotel. Pick up the trail card at Rossweid or the Gondelbahn Rossweid and enjoy the 1.5 km, interactive adventure with the children. The ground may be wet, so bring waterproof gear.
+ Additional hiking options are available from the *Berghotel*.
+ This area is home to the Entelbuch UNESCO biosphere.
+ There is a lift that runs in this area if you feel like skipping the hike and heading directly to the playground. The lift accepts *Halbtax* and the Junior Card.
+ In the winter try night sledding for the ultimate adventure!

Be Aware

+ Due to the small pond at the *Berghotel*, our children became quite wet and dirty. Bring extra clothes (or bathing clothes) and waterproof shoes.
+ No water on route to the *Berghotel*, though the route is short.
+ There is a toilet at the bus stop, the lift station and the *Berghotel*.
+ The hike up is steep, so take your time and assist children when necessary.

J F M A M J J A S O N D

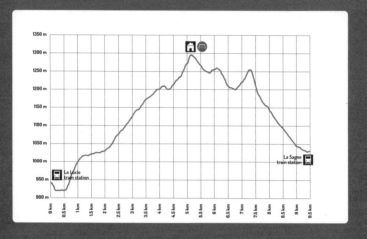

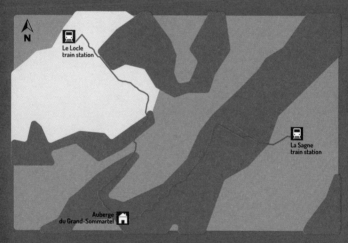

 Playground

Time for Winter

START
Le Locle
(train station)

FINISH
La Sagne
(train station)

🏠	↔	↗	↘	⋀	⚙
1292 m	9.5 km	500 m	404 m	1294 m	T1

↔ 5.2 km	🕐 2:50 h	↔ 4.3 km	🕐 1:50 h
Day 1		**Day 2**	
↗ 406 m	↘ 41 m	↗ 94 m	↘ 363 m

Auberge
du Grand-Sommartel

Overview

Once in Le Locle marvel at the fact that you are now visiting the epicenter of Swiss watchmaking. While in town, consider a visit to the Le Locle Watch Museum, "Musée D'Horlogerie Du Locle Chateau des Monts" to learn more about this town's rich watch history. This town, and its neighbour La-Chaux-de-Fonds, are listed as a UNESCO World Heritage Site.

After you leave the town, appreciate this unhurried and easy-going hike through the Jura Mountains. This track provides the perfect opportunity for families to spend quality time in nature year-round. With rolling hills and well-marked trails, the area is the ideal way to break up the winter. Once at the auberge, order cups of warm coffee and hot chocolate and prepare for the evening meal. Sleds are located outside of the dormitory, and with permission from the owners, children can take advantage of the perfect sledding hill that sits right in front of the house. As the sun rises, make your way down to the town of La Sagne through forests and winding trails. A train awaits in the town of La Sagne, but plan your departure in advance.

Directions

Day 1

With your back to the front of the Le Locle train station, take the funicular (on your right) down into the town. This will drop you off at the corner of Crêt-Perrelet and Rue de la Côte. Cross Rue de la Côte and take the next left down Rue du Temple. There is a Coop market approximately 60 m farther. Continue along Rue du Temple, turning right on Rue du Pont. Proceed down Rue du Pont for approximately 150 m (or three streets). There is a walkway heading up the hill that points the way with blue signs to the pool *(piscine – patinoire)*. This walkway will wander up the hill, crossing several streets heading to the community pool, located along Route du Communal. At the pool, the trail markers become visible. Proceed down Route du Communal, the trail will veer right into the forest after the field. The trail continues in and out of the forest, and will turn left at a farm shed. The auberge is just under 1 km up the trail through the forest.

Day 2

At the trail sign in front of the auberge, follow the trail in the direction of La Sagne, which will lead through a field. This is a pleasant walk through the forest that will, after 2.7 km, arrive at a road. Use caution crossing the street, as the road bends and cars may not have full visibility. Proceed down the dirt path, turning right just after the trees, approximately 120 m off the main road. The path will lead downhill, through the forest, parallel to the road, and then merge with the road at a farm. Follow the road (Le Crêt) into the town of La Sagne, turning right onto the road of the train station (Gare). The trail signs will point to La Sagne Crêt 5 m.

Trail Markers

Day 1
Le Locle Gare **»** Le Communal **»** Grand Som Martel (auberge)

Day 2
Grand Som Martel (auberge) **»** La Rocheta **»** La Sagne **»** La Sagne Crêt

Accommodation Overview

This auberge provides a functional dormitory for an evening away. The innkeepers serve your meals in a lively dining room with a child-friendly atmosphere. The sleeping quarter is a row of 16 bunk beds in a very tidy, efficient space. The views from the auberge are impressive and the children will be quite happy to pick up a sled and make the most of the winter snow.

Acommodation Details

Auberge du Grand-Sommartel
2314 La Sagne / contact@grand-sommartel.ch / +41 32 931 17 27
www.grand-sommartel.ch / GPS: 47.02771, 6.75885

+ The auberge (hostel) offers 16 beds in a single room; sleep sacks required
+ There is one shared toilet and two shared showers
+ No heat in the room
+ Electricity and outlets in the room
+ No Wi-Fi
+ Moderate cellular connectivity
+ À la carte menu. Vegetarian options available
+ Cash and credit cards accepted

Kid Approved

+ There are sledding and winter sport opportunities along the route and at the auberge.
+ This is an easy trail for hiking with children year-round.
+ There is a small playground on site during the summer months.
+ The house provides children's menus.

Tip

Bring a spare pair of shoes, as the auberge doesn't provide house shoes, or at least not during our visit. This is particularly helpful if your boots are wet from the snow and you are going up to the main house for dinner.

Special Features

+ This route offers views of rolling hills without having to put forth too much physical effort.
+ This is a fun winter escape and is ideal for snowshoeing during the winter months.
+ The auberge is open year-round.
+ Once you arrive at the auberge, the views of the Alps on a clear day are quite spectacular.
+ Don't forget to catch the sunrise at the auberge!

Be Aware

+ There are no toilets along the route.
  Use the toilet before exiting the train.
+ Stop in the town of Le Locle to purchase snacks or lunch and enjoy a picnic along the trail.
+ No water filling opportunities along the trail.
  Pack plenty of water for the entire route.
+ Sunglasses and sunscreen are a must for snow reflection and sun.
+ The first section of this hike is along a road. Proceed with caution and pay close attention to children.
+ There is no heat in the dormitory. Bring warm clothing and sleep sacks.

| J | F | M | A | M | J | J | A | S | O | N | D |

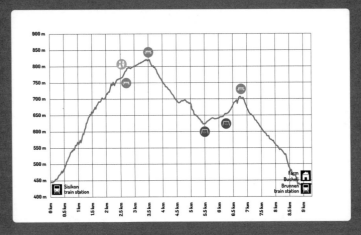

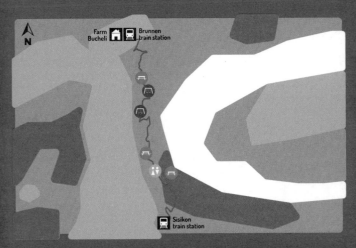

 Picnic / Grilling

Playground

Toilet

SZ
FARM BUCHELI

A Night on Straw

START
Sisikon
(train Station)

FINISH
Brunnen
(train Station)

| 437 m | 9.1 km | ↗ 500 m | ↘ 506 m | ⋀ 823 m | T1 |

Day 1		Day 2	
⊢⊣ 8.5 km	🕐 5:15 h	⊢⊣ 0.6 km	🕐 0:20 h
↗ 498 m	↘ 504 m	↗ 2 m	↘ 2 m

Farm Bucheli

Overview

The pleasant, yet gradual climb from Sisikon offers views of lake Urnersee, which are captivating and provide motivation during the first stretch of this hike. Three kilometers into the hike, you will discover an inviting place to grill or eat a picnic lunch. Take advantage of this covered area and use this time to refuel before pressing on. There are a few play areas along the route, located in Mättli and Morschach. These destinations break up the hike and allow the children sufficient play time.

Once at the farm, your children will be so immersed with animals and the farm operations that you might just have to beg them to wash-up before dinner and bed. Sleeping on straw is a unique opportunity and one that must be realized at least once in your lifetime. This adventure will be a family talking point for years to come.

Directions

Day 1

From the Sisikon train station with your back to the lake, turn right. You should see the Wanderweg signpost approximately 50 m ahead. Turn left, following signs toward "Binzenegg, Morschach, Brunnen." The path will weave through a residential area and parallel a stream on your left. The path will cross the stream and continue uphill through a forest and fields (for the next 3 km) until you reach a road. Use caution as the trail continues right, up the road for approximately 50 m before turning left back through the forest. At approximately 3 km, there is a covered picnic area with a grill. There is a toilet approximately 60 m past the picnic area, and a small self-serve store with seasonal farm products. The trail continues along fields, veering left at Schilti, descending along a road. Just past a small white church (Franz-Xaver-Kapelle), there is a sign post with multiple trail markers. We recommend turning left at this post in the direction of Mattli/Morschach/Brunnen, or else you will miss the swing as described below. This takes you past the Marienkappelle, down through a forest, and turns right onto a dirt road. Pay attention: when you merge onto the paved road, in the field to the left, is a fantastic two-person swing (Partnerschaukel). This is a great stopping point for the whole family.

Continue along the road toward Morschach (Caution: not Brunnen!) The trail sign post will be visible on a telephone pole. There will be a farm (Fronalp) with ponies, goats and cows, just before a race track in Morschach. Turn right at the main road continuing toward Morschach, and then left to cross the road at the self-serve tourist information kiosk. After crossing, you will see a large trail marker; follow the signs toward Axenstein/Brunnen. After 150 m there is a small playground, and the trail will continue up through a residential area. At Axenstein, there will be a picnic/grill station approximately 20 m to the right, but the path to follow will continue straight to Ingenbohler Wald/Brunnen. At the next sign post (Ingenbohler Wald), continue toward Kloster Ingenbohl/Brunnen. This will continue to meander through the forest and will open up to the front face of the Kloster Ingenbohl. The path will continue down a series of stairs, the farm will be at the bottom of the stairs. Follow the signs *Anmeldung* to the main house to check in.

Day 2

From the farm, proceed to the Brunnen train station. The direction is to the left as you come down the stairs from the day before. Just past the barn, the trail will fork; turn right toward the Brunnen train station. The path with zig-zag through several streets and to an underpass leading into the train station.

Trail Markers

Day 1

Sisikon ≫ Binzenegg ≫ Schilti ≫ Mattli ≫ Morschach ≫ Axenstein ≫ Ingenbohler Wald ≫ Kloster Ingenbohl ≫ Farm Bucheli

Day 2

Farm Bucheli ≫ Brunnen (Bahnhof)

Accommodation Overview

This is a working farm with lots of farm animals. You will be sleeping in a designated barn with other families. The barn is clean, spacious and designed to house guests for overnight stays. The farm provides thick wool blankets to place over the hay, but guests must bring their own sleeping bags. A toilet is located outside the barn, but in close proximity to the sleeping quarters. There are two bathrooms, with communal showers. Breakfast is offered as part of the rate (fresh bread, cheese, butter, jam, eggs, coffee, juice and hot chocolate); however, dinner is essentially on your own, unless you request this meal prior to your arrival. There is, however, a grill pit with picnic benches onsite where families can cook their dinner, should you feel inclined. The town of Brunnen is within walking distance from the farm and offers plenty of meal options, including grocery stores.

Acommodation Details

Farm Sleep on Straw — Familie Bucheli
6440 Ingenbohl-Brunnen / +41 41 820 06 70
www.schlafimstroh-bucheli.ch / GPS: 46.99826, 8.61423

+ Dormitory only; sleep sacks required
+ Shared bathrooms with showers
+ No heat available in the barn
+ Electricity and outlets in the barn
+ No Wi-Fi
+ Good cellular connectivity
+ Basic meal options available upon request
+ Cash only accepted

Kid Approved

+ The incredible swing at Mattli and the small playground in Morschach are true delights.
+ The gorgeous and child-friendly farm in Morschach invites you to walk in and say "hello" to the horses, ponies and cows. Notice the cows get to listen to music. Lucky cows!
+ In Morschach, the Swiss Holiday Park offers older children (8+) the opportunity to drive on the outdoor race car track (kartbahn), for more information visit: www.swissholidaypark.ch
+ Consider a visit to the Swiss Knife Valley Visitor Center in Brunnen, where the entire family will learn about the history and how to make Swiss Army Knives. The Visitor Center is located within walking distance from the farm and full of interesting information.

Tips

Tessa
If you want an ice cream, try and behave on the hike.

Noah
If you want to have a long sleep and a good sleep, bring a warm sleeping bag.

Special Features

+ The hike from Sisikon to Brunnen is beautiful.
+ Much of this route is through forests, offering a bit of shade during hot days and protection on rainy days.
+ You will be hiking on a portion of the "Swiss Path," national route 99, which officially starts in Rütli and ends in Brunnen taking hikers along 35 km of gorgeous hiking paths with markers denoting the year in which individual cantons joined Switzerland.
+ At the Schmid Farm, there is a small honesty shop (customer integrity at its finest) with: cheese, sausage, drinks, dried apples, honey and jam for sale. If you need picnic provisions at the grilling station, you can walk up to the Schmid Farm to purchase some food.
+ Sleeping on straw is an inexpensive overnight experience.
+ Sleeping on straw, come on, what a cool thing to do!

Be Aware

+ The hike from Sisikon to Brunnen is relatively long with a steady climb for the first hour or so. Plan an entire day to complete the hike.
+ The barn is not heated and can get cold; bring warm sleeping bags.
+ You will be staying on a working farm with: cows, calves, cats, rabbits, and chickens.
+ Bring earplugs for your overnight stay.
+ Bring a flashlight for using the toilet at night.

J F M A M J J A S O N D

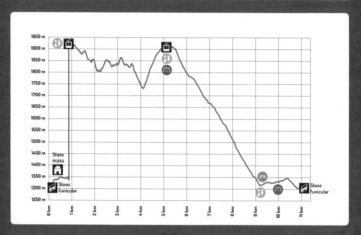

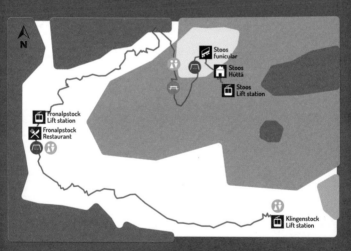

Picnic / Grilling

Playground

Toilet

Ridgelines and Moors

START
Stoos
(funicular)

FINISH
Stoos
(funicular)

1372 m	9.8 km	429 m	1011 m	1930 m	T2

4.4 km	2 h	4.2 km	1:45 h	1.2 km	1:30 h
Hike 1		**Hike 2**		**Hike 3**	
345 m	366 m	8 m	590 m	76 m	55 m

Stoos Hüttä

Overview

Stoos Hütta is the ideal site to explore the Stoos area. What makes this region so extraordinary is its remote and secluded location. Far away from cars and the hustle and bustle of everyday life, this is a peaceful retreat.

The three hikes we outline in this area are so picturesque you might want to consider a couple of nights for additional exploration. We completed hikes 1 and 2 the first day of our arrival. The third hike was completed early in the morning the second day of our visit. Though not necessarily a hike to a hut, the Stoos Hütta will require you to walk uphill for 10–15 minutes from the funicular and will be your base camp for the duration of your stay.

Fun fact: The funicular up to Stoos is a recent addition to the mountain. With a 110 % gradient, this just so happens to be the steepest funicular in the world. Wow! That is one serious engineering feat! The funicular was completed in December of 2017. Enjoy the ride and don't forget to look down to appreciate the steep journey!

Directions

Hike 1

Ridgeline from Klingenstock to Fronalpstock
This incredibly scenic hike offers incomprehensible views of Vierwaldstättersee (Lake Lucerne) and layered mountains in the distance. With attention and focus, experienced hiking families can enjoy this ridgeline hike. Be aware of sharp drops on both sides of the trail, and steep ascents and descents. Check the lift operating times, as the lift may not be operating until June. Being able to rely on the Klingenstock lift is a must with children!

Directions Hike 1 (4.4 km)
The most challenging of the three hikes begins at the top of the Klingenstock lift station. Exit the lift station heading right, toward Fronalpstock. The trail will undulate over the ridgeline and between several peaks and is easy to navigate to Fronalpstock. The last climb from Furggeli to Fronalpstock will zig-zag uphill, slowly levelling out, until the beautiful alpine playground at Fronalpstock comes into view, a short distance from the Gipfel Fronalpstock Restaurant. The people who own and operate this restaurant are incredible. Please enjoy a meal at the restaurant.

Hike 2

Descending Fronalpstock
Oh, this area is a visual wonder. If you are starting your journey with this hike, don't forget to stop at the entertaining playground at Fronalpstock. Take your time moving slowly through this downhill trail, taking in the views and the fresh air. It is a relatively easy trail to navigate, providing additional views of the lake and the local mountains. Cast your gaze across the valley to see small and big Mythen.

Directions Hike 2 (4.2 km)

This hike maybe combined with hike 1. This is a moderate hike from Fronalpstock down to Stoos. From the Fronalpstock lift station (if you elect to go by lift), exit the lift and walk around the right side of the Fronalpstock Restaurant when facing it. The trail will lead toward Charenstöckli. Keep left when the trail splits, this route will provide you with a wonderful view of the lake. Continue toward Mettlen, which will zig-zag down near the bottom of the lift, depositing you at the edge of Stoos. Continue through the village and back up to the Stoos Hüttä to complete the hike.

Hike 3

The Moor

This is the perfect way to end your journey in Stoos. Grab the theme trail brochure on the way into the moor and allow your children the opportunity to explore at their own pace. If you are inclined, enjoy a foot plunge in the small lake as you start this hike. This is an easy trail to navigate.

Directions Hike 3 (1.2 km)

From the small Stoos lake, (Stoos-Seeli) walk past the lake and water play area. There is picnic/grill area and a small farm located on the path that sells cheese, yogurt, honey and meat. This simple loop and theme trail, "Moorerlebnis" path, has several stations along the path, part of which is on an elevated wooden walkway. The trail aims to educate you on the interesting ecosystems of the moor.

Trail Markers

Hike 1
Klingenstock ≫ Furggeli ≫ Fronalpstock

Hike 2
Fronalpstock ≫ Charenstöckli ≫ Mettlen ≫ Stoos

Hike 3
Moorerlebnis path

Accommodation Overview

The Stoos Hüttä is perched on a hill with lovely views. This stylish hut is perfect for making a full weekend of hiking in the Stoos area. With rooms that accommodate small and large families, including private bathrooms and towering bunk beds, this family-friendly spot is a relaxing retreat. The evening meal is a genuine affair offering delicious food in a snug dining area. Enjoy!

The majority of this hut was built with local wood, making it an extremely special and a beautifully crafted place to stay. Each room in the hut was named after a tree, which is inscribed on each bedroom door. It was evident that love and attention went into the creation of this hut.

Accommodation Details

Stoos Hüttä
6433 Stoos / info@stooshutta.ch / +41 41 818 08 60
www.stooshutta.ch / GPS: 46.97527, 8.67027

+ Private rooms with sheets, duvets and towels provided
+ Private bathroom with showers in the rooms
+ Heat in the room
+ Electricity and outlets in the room
+ Free Wi-Fi
+ Good cellular connectivity
+ Vegetarian options available, request at the time of booking
+ Cash and credit cards accepted

Kid Approved

+ There is a modest playground onsite at the hut.
+ The bunk beds at the hut are very high, which can be a source of incredible joy for little people! Use caution when climbing the ladder with smaller children.
+ The "Moorerlebnisweg" theme trail has interactive stations through the peaceful moor. There is a water play area, a small lake and the opportunity to stamp your brochure at each of the eight stations visited.
+ The incredible alpine playground at Fronalpstock is as gorgeous as are the views!

Tip

Drop your bags off at the Stoos Hüttä and carry only what you need for a successful day on the trails. Pack plenty of water, snacks, your medical kit, layers for warmth, a harness for your child (if you use one) and your wallet. By leaving your pack at the hut, the ridgeline hike will be easier to navigate.

Wo versteckt sich
der Grasf[...]
auf der ande[...]

Der Grasfrosch

In der Schweiz ist der Grasfrosch der am häufigst[...]
auftretende Froschlurch. Der sieben bis zehn Zentimeter gr[...]
Grasfrosch besiedelt Grünland, Biotope, Gebüsche, Ge[...]ufer,
Wälder, Gärten, Parks und Moore. Nachts gehen die Fr[...] auf Jagd
nach Insekten. Tagsüber verstecken sie sich an feuc[...] Plätzen.
Grasfrösche sind begehrte Beutetiere für Störche, [...],
Raubvögel, Ringelnattern, Forellenfische, Wild[...]eine,
Füchse, Dachse, Iltise und Wanderratte[...]

Special Features

+ A beautiful location, making a great hub for one or more overnights.
+ The hikes are all special in their own right and offer remarkable views throughout.
+ There are plenty of playgrounds and child-friendly opportunities in this area.

Be Aware

+ We completed all of the hikes during the autumn months, but the Klingenstock to Fronalpstock should never be attempted in poor weather conditions.
+ Be aware that the route from Klingenstock to Fronalpstock can be busy with hikers. Plan accordingly, but don't miss this stunning hike.
+ The hut is located on a hill and will require back and forth coming and going. Be prepared to hike back to the hut each day.
+ Bring a nightlight or flashlight for navigating the steep stairs of the bunk beds.
+ Toilets are available at the first lift station in Klingenstock, Fronalpstock, Stoos-Seeli, and the funicular station.
+ Even though the hut is open in winter, most of the hiking trails are not accessible.

| J | F | M | A | M | J | J | A | S | O | N | D |

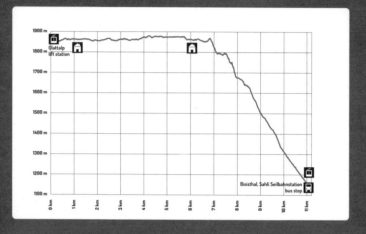

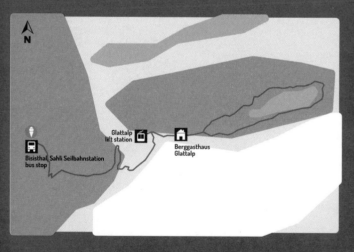

 Ice cream

SZ
BERGGASTHAUS GLATTALP

Up
the Last Valley!

17

START
Glattalp
(lift station)

FINISH
Bisisthal, Sahli Seilbahnstat.
(bus stop)

| 1856 m | 11.2 km | 145 m | 852 m | 1870 m | T2 |

6.2 km	3 h		5 km	2 h
Day 1			**Day 2**	
105 m	111 m		40 m	741 m

Berggasthaus
Glattalp

Overview

This area is so remote that it almost feels as though it could be the last valley in canton Schwyz[1]. Once you make your way up to Glattalp, you will see what the canton is hiding, as the area reveals a high pasture in a long valley with a picturesque lake. This area urges you to slow down, disconnect, and maybe even take a nap in the grass by the lake. Life moves at a slower place here, and that's necessary in our fast-paced world.

Directions

Day 1
Exit the Glattalp lift station and follow the trail to the right in the direction of Glattalpsee. The Berggasthaus Glattalp will be on your left just 700 m away. Have a snack and/or ask to drop off your bags as you begin your journey of touring the lake. Farther down the trail, past the *Berggasthaus*, you will arrive at Glattalp/Seeloch. You can choose to loop the lake in either direction, arriving back at the same point. When walking around the lake from the right side (when facing the lake), there are two trails, an upper and lower trail. Both will lead you to the back of the lake, Glattalpsee/Seeboden. Keep in mind that the lower trail may be immersed in water in the early part of the season. Make your way back to the *Berggasthaus* for the night.

Day 2
In the morning, a walk down to Sahli should not be missed. Although the trail will be steep at times, it is a well-marked, wide path that is used to migrate livestock. This path may be challenging at times while walking down, due to the loose rocks. Make your way on to Läcki, and then to Sahli, which is the lower lift station. On your way down you will be walking through pastures with sheep and cows. Past Läcki, the trail will follow a road down; use caution, as cars are active in summer months. The road will arrive at the parking area and the lift station Sahli. The bus stop is located at the lift station.

Trail Markers

Day 1
Glattalp >> Bergwirtschaft Glattalp >> Glattalp/Seeloch >> Glattalpsee/Seeboden >> Glattalp/Seeloch >> Bergwirtschaft Glattalp

Day 2
Bergwirtschaft Glattalp >> Läcki >> Sal

---

1   The area feels so secluded that you cannot help but think you have hiked to the last valley in Schwyz. If you do happen to find the last valley, let us know!

Accommodation Overview

Berggasthaus Glattalp is a quaint mountain house situated in a shallow, yet scenic valley. The friendly staff is pleased to serve you and encourages you to slow down and unwind. The area is calm and it is a great place to disconnect from the commotion of the world.

Acommodation Details

Berggasthaus Glattalp

6436 Bisisthal / gruezi@berggasthaus-glattalp.com / +41 41 830 12 04
www.berggasthaus-glattalp.com / GPS: 46.91543, 8.88201

+ Dormitories and several double rooms; sleep sack required
+ Shared bathrooms without showers
+ No heat in the rooms
+ Electricity and outlets in the rooms
+ No Wi-Fi
+ Weak cellular connectivity
+ Dinner is a fixed menu, request vegetarian options in advance
+ Cash only

Kid Approved

Frogs, newts, cows, and sheep! Wow!

Tips

Tessa
Watch where you step in the grass; there are frogs!

Parents
Put down your phone and relax! There are few places left in this world that are this tranquil. Enjoy.

Special Features

+ The route has one large lake and several smaller lakes. In the sunlight, the lakes look green, and may contain frogs in early summer.
+ This hike feels incredibly faraway and peaceful. What a welcome treat!
+ This is one of the coldest locations in Switzerland during the winter months and the snow levels can be very deep. When you hike, notice the unusually tall hiking signposts! Point them out to your children, they might just find this humorous.
+ For those who appreciate geology, this area is a great example of anticline and syncline rock formations. Check out all those layers! Did you know the area of Muotathal is home to the longest and deepest cave systems in Europe? With over 207 km of length and over 1,000 m of elevation difference, this is quite an impressive cave system. Keep your eyes open as you hike, there are other interesting rock formations caused by the limestone in the area.

Be Aware

+ In the early season, the main trail to the right of the lake (when facing it) may be under water. There is an upper, parallel trail, which you can be used to by-pass flooded trails.
+ The lift is small (8 person) and may be busy on nice summer days. If you plan to walk up to Glattalp, be prepared for a steep hike!
+ There are toilets at the lift station and the *Berggasthaus*.
+ It is advised to call the *Berggasthaus* when you make your reservation.
+ Berggasthaus Glattalp is small and snug. If you are looking for an alternative accommodation in the area, Glattalphütte SAC is on the hill above the lift station. It underwent renovations in 2020.
+ The route around the lake is easy, but the path down to Sahli may be hard on the knees, so bring hiking poles.
+ The lift station at Glattalp does not accept *Halbtax* or Junior Cards, for more information: www.stoos-muotatal.ch
+ Spelling of Sali (hiking signs) and Sahli (bus stop) are different.

J F M A M J J A S O N D

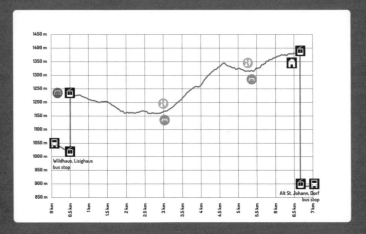

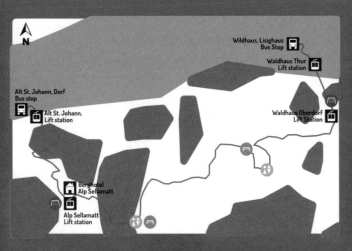

 Picnic / Grilling

Playground

Toilet

SG
BERGHOTEL ALP SELLAMATT

A Lake
and Bells

18

START
Wildhaus, Lisighaus
(bus stop)

FINISH
Alt St. Johann, Dorf
(bus stop)

1400 m	9.5 km	309 m	604 m	1400 m	T1

6.4 km	3 h		3.1 km	1:15 h
Day 1			**Day 2**	
309 m	143 m		0 m	501 m

**Berghotel
Alp Sellamatt**

Overview

This route is particularly lovely with all the wild flowers in bloom in the late spring. The photogenic Schwendisee (lake), which provides grills and dramatic views. Take your time on this route, as it is meant to be enjoyed slowly. Children will remain motivated as this trail overlaps part of the sound theme trail ("Klangweg").

Relax as the evening unfolds in the rustic hotel with a four-course meal before you head off for a peaceful night's rest. The next morning, appreciate the breakfast buffet before you make your way down the mountain.

Directions

Day 1

From the bus stop Wildhaus, Lisighaus, follow the signs in the direction of Wildhaus Talstation, by turning right down Vordere Schwendistrasse. This will meander down to the lift station (Wildhaus Talstation), which you can take to the top to Berggasthaus Oberdorf. This is a great place to enjoy a bite to eat and let the children play. The trail veers to your right as you leave the *Berggasthaus* (or the lift station). Follow signs toward Schwendiseen, and make your way around the lake. There are multiple grilling stations and benches here to enjoy a picnic. Once around the lake, continue along the road to Iltios. The trail continues through a field, part of a forest, and past another grilling area. The trail will zig-zag uphill; you will turn right onto the road, and follow it approximately 1 km to Berghotel Sellamatt.

Day 2

From Berghotel Sellamatt, you can take the lift down to Alt St. Johann, or hike down. To hike down, follow the signs (next to the lift station across from Berghotel Sellamatt) down toward Alt St. Johann. The trail will lead downhill, running parallel to the lift. At the signpost Chueweid, you will turn right into the forest. The trail will veer left while in the forest and then turn right again just before exiting the forest. The trail turns left one last time, and the lift station will be just below you with the lift cable overhead.

Trail Markers

Day 1

Lisighaus ≫ Seeselbahn Talstation ≫ Oberdorf ≫ Schwendiseen ≫ Iltios ≫ Selamatt

Day 2

Selamatt ≫ Chueweid ≫ Alt St. Johann

Accommodation Overview

Berghotel Sellamatt is located within view of the Alpstein Massif. With plenty of trails located directly in front of the house, this location is ideal for hikers and active families. The staff members at the hotel are very accommodating and the four-course meal is served with care. The *Berghotel* offers both dormitories and private rooms. Private rooms include all bed linens and a private bathroom with shower. Sleep sacks and towels are required for dormitory accommodations.

Acommondation Details

Berghotel Alp Sellamatt
9656 Alt St. Johann / berghotel@sellamatt.ch / +41 71 999 13 30
www.sellamatt.ch / GPS: 47.18249, 9.29682

+ Private family rooms available with sheets, duvets and towels
+ Dormitories available; sleep sacks required
+ Heat in the rooms
+ Electricity and outlets in the rooms
+ Free Wi-Fi
+ Good cellular reception
+ Fixed menu. Vegetarian options available, request at the time of booking
+ Cash and credit cards accepted

Kid Approved

Part of this trail includes a few of the stations included in the "Klangweg" or sound trail theme route, which, when completed in its entirety, includes 27 stations.

Tip

Try the local beer (Churfirsten Bier) at the Berggasthaus Oberdorf. Stretch your legs and relax on the terrace while the children play at the playground.

Special Features

+ The children's playground at Berggasthaus Oberdorf is fun.
+ Schwendisee (lake) is a scenic location for grilling.
+ A toilet is located at the lake and at the second grill station past Iltios.
+ Access to lifts can make the route easier.
+ The entertaining "Klangweg" is open from May through October.
+ The area celebrates a bell festival each year in May. At the festival, you can learn about, hear, take lessons, and make bells.
  For more information visit www.klangwelt.swiss
+ Food and toilets are available at both Berggasthaus Oberdorf and Bergrestaurant Iltios.

Be Aware

+ No water available along the route, except at the *Berghotels*.
+ Both of the lifts accept the *Halbtax* and the Junior Card. The lift from Alt. St. Johann to Alp Sellamatt runs from early June through the middle of October. For more information visit: www.chaeserrugg.ch and www.wildhaus.ch
+ If driving you can park your car at the base of Alt St. Johann lift station and take the bus to Wildhaus Lisighaus bus stop.
+ Spelling of Selamatt (hiking signs) and Sellamatt *(Berghaus)* are different.

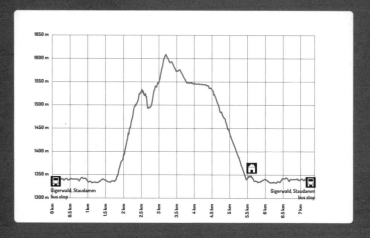

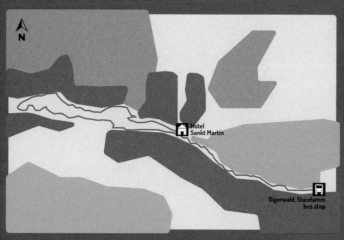

SG
HOTEL SANKT MARTIN

Historical Hamlet

START
Gigerwald, Staudamm
(bus stop)

FINISH
Gigerwald, Staudamm
(bus stop)

1351 m	14.4 km	309 m	604 m	1612 m	T2

10.9 km	3:20 h		3.5 km	1:20 h
Day 1			**Day 2**	
391 m	380 m		36 m	22 m

Restaurant & Hotel
Sankt Martin

Overview

The bus will drop you off at the massive dam at Gigerwaldsee. Make your way carefully along the road, through a tunnel until you arrive at the small cluster of buildings known as St. Martin. Drop off your bags, take a while to soak in the historical nature of the area and make your way to the back of the valley. The hike is relatively easy, as it undulates throughout the duration of the route. The views are plentiful and the waterfalls are many. As you walk, consider the history of St. Martin and try to imagine what life was like all those years ago for those that resided in the region.

Though most areas within Switzerland carry a unique charm, this area is extremely special and rich with history. Dating back to 1312, this tiny hamlet was originally home to twelve families and roughly one hundred people, despite its remote, almost inhospitable location.

The petite chapel on site was constructed in 1312 and visited by priests to perform religious ceremonies a few times per year. In the mid 1600s, the families had all left the area with the exception of Ursula Sutter who despite her move to Vättis, would return during the summer months. As all the people abandoned this miniature village, the area returned to a mountain and forest region once again. The people that had once inhabited this spot fled for multiple reasons, one of which was how hard it was to maintain daily life due to its geographical positioning and thus, the area, after years of deforestation, became subject to avalanches and run off, which are still active to this day. The little settlement has exchanged hands over the years; however, it still maintains its history and captivating allure.

Walking through the small area, one can only envision the harshness of life hundreds of years ago. Now with an access road and modern-day conveniences, this remote location is a true haven for hungry hikers and those seeking relaxation.

Directions

Day 1

From the Gigerwald, Staudamm bus stop, head in the direction of St. Martin. Use caution as the road is shared with cars and will lead through a long tunnel. At the end of the lake, the trail will curve right, past a parking area on your left. You will see the hotel just up the hill on your right. Consider having a snack and/or dropping your bags off at the hotel. This trail begins at the end of the main parking lot (which you passed upon arrival), not the parking lot next to Sankt Martin Hotel. The trail will head up stream toward Tüfwald with the river on your right. The trail will continue uphill through the forest, past a waterfall, and emerge at a field. Tüfwald is at the top of the field. Continue downhill toward Hintere Ebni/Sardonaalp. The trail will begin to head uphill and cross several small streams. Use caution as the streams have eroded in the area where the trail has been re-routed. The path will arrive at Vordere Ebni, a large open field with several houses. There is a sign on a fence marked "Fahr und Fussweg nach St. Martin." Take the path/dirt road to the right leading in the direction of St. Martin. This road will connect with the main road which is a marked trail back to St. Martin.

Day 2

From St. Martin hike to the parking lot and continue on the road in the direction of Gigerwald. Use caution when walking along this road.

Trail Markers

Day 1

Staumauer Gigerwald >> St. Martin >> Tüfwald >> Vordere Ebni >> St. Martin

Day 2

St. Martin >> Staumauer Gigerwald

Accommodation Overview

What a remarkable escape positioned in the Calfeisental Valley. The main house has been beautifully restored, making an overnight stay a timeless escape. The food is lovingly prepared and delivered. Enjoy an evening by the fire, with a glass of wine, plenty of conversation and a good game.

Acommondation Details

Restaurant & Hotel Sankt Martin
7315 Vättis / info@sanktmartin.ch / +41 81 306 12 34
www.sanktmartin.ch / GPS: 46.92072, 9.35727

+ Private rooms available with sheets, duvets and towels
+ Shared bathrooms and showers
+ Heat in the rooms
+ Electricity and outlets in the room
+ Free Wi-Fi
+ Moderate cellular connectivity
+ Fixed menu. Vegetarian options available, request at the time of booking
+ Cash and credit cards accepted

Tip

Try the St. Martin Chilchli beer after the hike. It's a refreshing treat!

Special Features

+ The St. Martin area dates back to 1312, making it rich with history.
+ The church onsite was placed under protection after
  its restoration in 1955.
+ There is a hot pot and sauna, which are available for a fee.
+ Easy access to trails from the hotel.
+ E-bikes available at the hotel.
+ Part of the UNESCO World Heritage Site Tectonic Arena Sardona.

Be Aware

+ Use caution when hiking along the road during
  the first portion of this route.
+ There are no real child-centric activities at this location, but both
  nature and history are plentiful. Consider making the most of chapter
  four for child-centric ideas to keep your little people happy.
+ No drinking water along the route.
+ No toilets along the route.
+ No snacks available along the route, pack plenty.
+ Some areas of the hiking route may be subject to wash out during
  winter months and heavy rains. Use caution in these areas and assist
  children. The trail may be rerouted around such areas.
+ If driving, please know the access road to St. Martin is accessible
  for 20 minutes each direction, alternating times throughout the day.
  The road is extremely narrow, oftentimes wet and shared with hikers.
  If driving, please pay close attention to the posted driving times and
  be aware of hikers along the route. Also know the height of the driving
  route is limited to 2.6 meters.

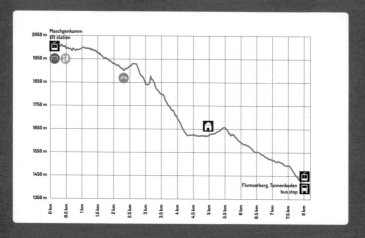

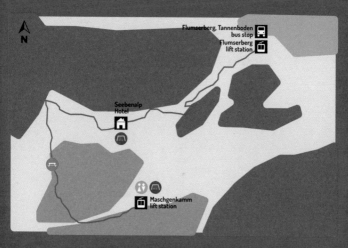

Picnic / Grilling

Playground

Toilet

SG
BERGHOTEL SEEBENALP

Ridgelines
and Lakes

START
Maschgenkamm
(lift station)

FINISH
Flumserberg, Tannenboden
(bus stop)

1620 m	8 km	193 m	786 m	2074 m	T2

4.9 km	2:25 h	3.1 km	1:10 h
Day 1		**Day 2**	
157 m	509 m	36	277

Berghotel
Seebenalp

Overview

The Flumserberg area is particularly attractive with views that stretch in every direction. This striking ridgeline hike is at times demanding, but offers mountain and lake views throughout with a lovely descent down to the historic Seebenalp Berghotel. This hike is best appreciated in good weather and during the height of summer, when the snow has melted and the sun is sharing its warmth.

From the moment the children step off the lift at Maschgenkamm, they will want to spend plenty of time pulling themselves across the pond on the modest raft and searching for frogs. Once the fun has been had, make your way up the steep ridgeline (don't worry, it levels out relatively quickly) and take in the gorgeous sights. Once off the first ridgeline, there are plenty of benches and even an area for grilling to eat lunch before the next ridgeline begins. Take your time on this hike to admire the sights and to assist children. As you make your descent down to the hotel, you will once again get ready for another relaxing evening. Enjoy a cake on the terrace, check in to your room, and allow the children free time to play at the small play area at the hotel. For those still longing for additional walking routes, consider completing the loop around the lake (Grosssee).

Directions

Day 1
There are several routes to get to Seebenalp; the route we outline allows for spectacular views of the entire area. Exit the Maschgenkamm lift station. Opposite the small pond/play area, the ridgeline trail over the mountain Ziger is visible; this is a preferred route which offers commanding views of the area. If the ridgeline is not desirable, the level path to the right can also be used, as both routes will head toward Zigerfurgglen. At Zigerfurgglen, follow the sign "nach 60 m weiterer Wegweiser" and then toward Chrüzen. There is a grill/picnic area at Chrüzen. From Chrüzen, follow the signs toward Chli Güslen/Seebenalp, which offers fantastic ridgeline views. The trail will fork at Chli Güslen, turning right in the direction of Seebenalp and heading downhill. Be careful in this area by the streams, we found tiny leaf frogs in the wet grass area before the lake (Heusee). Follow the trail to the second lake (Grosssee) and around its bank to Berghotel Seebenalp.

Day 2
On the second day, head in the direction of Tannenbodenalp. This will take you along a mountain road. As you leave Seebenalp, can you find the stone that Obelix lost on his way to Rome? Continue along the road using caution as there may be cars. After approximately 2.5 km, the trail will turn left down through a field just before the Floomzer toboggan run. The trail will end on a road which is just across from the Tannenboden lift station, bus stop and parking area.

Trail Markers

Day 1
Maschgenkamm ≫ Zigerfurgglen ≫ Chrüzen ≫ Chli Güslen ≫ Heusee ≫ Seebenalp

Day 2
Seebenalp ≫ Winkelzan ≫ Rotberg ≫ Tannenboden

Accommodation Overview

This rustic old hotel is perched directly on Grosssee. The original hotel, from our understanding, was built in 1889 and sat near Heusee, but was destroyed by an avalanche. The hotel as it is currently situated, was rebuilt in the year 1907 and was used as a spa destination for those longing to breathe fresh mountain air. The rooms are simple and functional.

Acommondation Details

Berghotel Seebenalp
8884 Oberterzen / hotel.seebenalp@bluewin.ch / +41 81 738 12 23
www.seebenalp.ch / GPS: 47.08041, 9.24843

+ Private family rooms available with sheets, duvets and towels
+ Shared bathrooms and showers
+ Heat and a sink in the rooms
+ Electricity and outlets in the room
+ No Wi-Fi
+ Good cellular connectivity
+ Fixed menu. Vegetarian options available, request at the time of booking
+ Cash and credit cards accepted

Kid Approved

+ The Floomzer toboggan run and the CLiiMBER Climbing Tower.
  For more information visit: www.flumserberg.ch
+ The play area located at Maschgenkamm.
+ The modest playground at the hotel.
+ The lakes in the area.

Tip

Tessa
In the summer months look out for tiny frogs on the trails. Also, in wet weather, be careful of the salamanders!

Special Features

+ The two ridgelines of this route are particularly
  beautiful, offering incredible views.
+ Child-friendly areas at the start and finish of this hike.
+ Lake views throughout.
+ The lift station accepts *Halbtax* and the Junior Card.
  For more information visit: www.flumserberg.ch
+ This hike can be made easier by bypassing the ridgeline.
+ UNESCO World Heritage Site Tectonic Arena Sardona.

Be Aware

+ There are two ridgelines to navigate on this route,
  so please pay close attention to sharp drop-offs.
+ Do not attempt the ridgeline route in poor weather conditions
  or in the winter months. If you plan to stay at the hotel in winter,
  hike in from Tannenboden (see directions Day 2 in reverse). In winter,
  the hotel is accessible by ski lifts in close proximity
  to the hotel and with snowshoes.
+ Harnesses and poles may be advisable on this route.
+ No drinking water or toilets available along the route.
+ Pack layers for this route. We were quite chilly in early September.
+ No overnight stays are possible on Sundays and the hotel closes
  at 18:00 during the summer months.

J	F	M	A	M	J	J	A	S	O	N	D

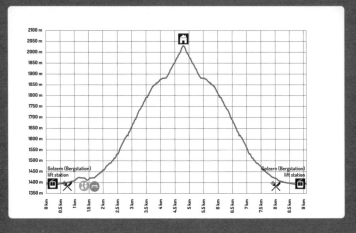

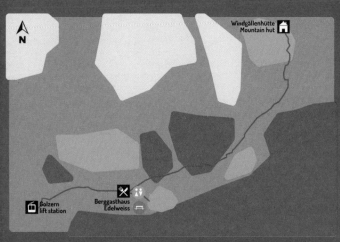

 Picnic / Grilling

 Toilet

A Gem in
the Mountains

START
Golzern (Bergstation)
(lift station)

FINISH
Golzern (Bergstation)
(lift station)

2032 m	9.1 km	791 m	759 m	2032 m	T2

4.8 km	3:10 h		4.3 km	2:50 h
Day 1			**Day 2**	
755 m	65 m		36 m	694 m

Windgällenhütte
AACZ

Overview

This area feels exceptional from the moment you exit the lift station. Tiny houses dot the landscape as you make your way down to the tranquil lake. Allow time for the children to play or swim before making your way up to the hut. The hike to Windgällenhütte is a slow climb, but use the distance to absorb the gorgeous surroundings. Play a game with the children, or refer to the "Get to Know You Questions" in chapter four to distract the group from all the climbing required to reach this remarkable hut.

Upon your arrival at the hut, the innkeepers whose smiles remain steady throughout your stay will welcome you with open arms. They had us at, "Would you like a welcome tea?" To which we quickly said, "Yes" and eased into the stunning surroundings. We couldn't wait to receive the hammer and chisel provided by the hut and got straight to work looking for crystals in the designated area. There is a recreational area below the hut that encourages guests to sit and relax or play a game of volleyball. This location is extraordinary, not only because of the nature and the impressive views, but also because of the warm smiles and pride the innkeepers emit throughout your stay. It is certain you will be swept away by the charm and the remote nature of the hut.

Directions

Day 1
Exit the lift station and walk toward Seewen along a road. This will lead past several clusters of houses and to the Golzerensee (lake) approximately 1.4 km from the lift station. From the lake, head back to Seewen, then take the trail to the right, which heads uphill in the direction of Windgällenhütte. This is a long, steady climb lasting almost 3 km. Windgällenhütte comes into view during the last 550 m.

Day 2
You can return to the Golzeren lift station the way you came. Note: There is an alternate way up to and from the hut, via Oberchäseren. The elevation profile is approximately the inverse of the recommended route with most of the climbing occurring in the first 1.8 km. The alternative route may not be ideal for some families, and is not recommend in wet weather.

Trail Markers

Day 1
Golzeren Bergstation ≫ Seewen ≫ Golzerensee ≫ Seewen ≫ Windgällenhütte

Day 2
Windgällenhütte ≫ Seewen ≫ Golzeren Bergstation

Accommodation Overview

This hut is something special, not only because of its remote, absolutely gorgeous location, but because of the innkeepers who pride themselves on making your stay memorable. The hut is impeccably clean, the meals are cooked with love and the dining room is warm and welcoming. When you visit this hut, you truly feel away from it all, and believe us, that is a very good thing!

Acommondation Details

Windgällenhütte AACZ (Akademischer Alpen Club Zürich)
6475 Bristen / info@windgaellenhuette.ch / +41 41 885 10 88
www.windgaellenhuette.ch / GPS: 46.79017, 8.75578

+ Private, modest bunk bedrooms; sleep sacks with pillowcases required
+ Shared bathroom without showers
+ Electricity, but no outlets in the room
+ No Wi-Fi
+ Weak cellular connectivity
+ Fixed menu. Vegetarian options available, request at the time of booking
+ Cash and credit cards accepted

Kid Approved

+ The lake in the beginning of the hike, which is fun for splashing,
  swimming and searching for frogs.
+ You can borrow a hammer and chisel to search
  for crystals in a designated location at the hut.
+ The opportunity to play volleyball or soccer and relax at
  the small "beach" area at the hut.
+ Depending on when you visit the hut, you might just be lucky enough
  to see the resident llamas.

Tips

Noah
If the weather is wet, look out for salamanders along the trail and watch where you step!

Parents
If you are lucky, you might just be able to experience alphorns and yodeling prior to drifting off to sleep. We were fortunate enough to hear both, making our stay extra special.

Special Features

+ The lake is a beautiful place to start the hike. In hot weather, bring a bathing suit and a small towel.
+ The area is gorgeous and void of tourism. Hooray!
+ The area is rich with crystals, which are available for sale along the trail.
+ During the hike, look for animals, such as chamois, salamanders, marmot, etc.
+ There are caves in close proximity to the hut. Ask the innkeepers, should you be interested in exploring the area further.

Be Aware

+ This hike is not advised in poor weather conditions.
+ There are no toilet facilities after the lake.
+ No water available along the route. Pack plenty.
+ There are lots of big rocks to navigate along the route. Help children with this and know the rocks may be slippery when wet.
+ This is a slow and steady uphill climb all the way to the hut. Take your time.
+ There are sinkholes approximately 100 m north of the hut. Watch children carefully in this area.
+ The lift station does not offer discounts of any kind. For more information visit www.lsb-golzern.ch
+ There is one outlet area available outside of the dining room at the hut to charge phones. Please make a donation for the service.
+ Please carry your trash with you from the hut.

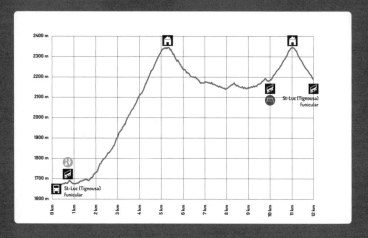

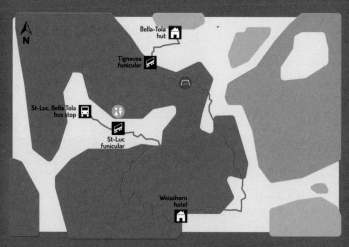

 228

Val d'Anniviers Tour

START
St-Luc "Tignousa"
(funicular)

FINISH
St-Luc "Tignousa"
(funicular)

⌂	⊢⊣	↗	↘	⋀	≡
2337 m / 2340 m	11.7 km	1011 m	492 m	2340 m	T1

⊢⊣ 4.9 km	🕐 2:15 h	⊢⊣ 5.7 km	🕐 3:20 h	⊢⊣ 1.1 km	🕐 0:25 h
Day 1		**Day 2**		**Day 3**	
↗ 711 m	↘ 15 m	↗ 285 m	↘ 291 m	↗ 15 m	↘ 186 m

Hotel Weisshorn

Cabane Bella-Tola

Overview

This three-day, two-night tour is a delight, though you will have to work to reach your first destination, which is Hotel Weisshorn. It is an uphill hike, which can be deceiving at only 4 km, so pace yourselves. The gift of this route is that it is primarily through forests and shaded. Once you arrive at the hotel, you will observe that its walls are tattered, the floorboards are creaky, but all of the old characteristics present a unique charm.

The next day, allow a full day to hike the planet theme trail, which starts just next to the hotel. Neptune will be your first planet to visit on this route. This hike is easy, though timely, with all of the planetary stops you will want to make. The planets will entice the children to keep hiking and encourage them to learn as they go. If time permits, stop at the planetarium in St-Luc and enjoy a talk by the local astronomer (at least during our visit), who is extremely passionate about his work. After a brief informational overview, you will have the opportunity to go up to the roof and safely view the sun through a high-powered telescope.

Continue on and up to your final destination, which will be Bella-Tola. This hut is a no-frills accommodation with friendly staff. With views that expand in the distance to the Matterhorn, pull up a seat on the lawn, take off your boots and enjoy a fresh, local blueberry pie.

Day three will be your easiest day. After breakfast, make you way down to the funicular and on to your final destination. Though your sore legs will long be forgotten, the memory of the views will last a long time.

Directions

Day 1
Proceed past the bottom funicular station of St-Luc (Tignousa) in the direction of Le Prilet / Hotel Weisshorn. The trail will veer right at Le Prilet continuing toward Hotel Weisshorn and Centre du Valais. This starts the long ascent, gaining approximately 700 m in 3 km, so take it easy. You will pass the geographic center of Valais within the first uphill kilometer, and a farm house with a picnic area near the second kilometer. After about nine switchbacks, the trees begin to thin, and the ground becomes a light sandy dirt. Hotel Weisshorn sits impressively just above you.

Day 2
You may notice the Neptune sculpture on the hill behind Hotel Weisshorn: The trails from the top of the hill are not marked and meander all over. The trail starts on the right of Hotel Weisshorn when you are facing the trail markers with the hotel behind them. Follow signs toward Toûno Le Chiesso, keeping left from the Neptune sculpture. Avoid the road as this is longer and less scenic. The trail will lead past a waterfall and past a large stream with a bench next to it. The trail continues past a farm house and reconnects with the road. The trail will continue to Tignousa approximately 3.5 km after the farmhouse. The trail will run along or parallel to the road. There is an observatory on the hill, above the trail, just before Tignousa. From Tignousa, the trail will continue up toward Cabane Bella-Tola via several switchbacks for another kilometer.

Day 3
From Cabane Bella-Tola, proceed down to Tignousa and take the funicular down to St-Luc.

Trail Markers

Day 1
St-Luc **》** Le Prilet **》** Hotel Weisshorn

Day 2
Hotel Weisshorn **》** Toûno Le Chiesso **》** Tignousa **》** Cabane Bella Tola

Day 3
Cabane Bella Tola **》** Tignousa

Accommodation Overview
for Hotel Weisshorn

Hotel Weisshorn rests high on a hill and maintains a very rustic charm. Sitting at 2,337 m, this hotel offers its guests superior views. Construction for this hotel was started in 1882 and completed approximately one year later. A few short years after its opening, the hotel was ravaged by a fire in 1889 and was thus rebuilt. The hotel feels rich with history, which is noticeable as you walk along the corridors.

Dinner is a lavish ordeal with four courses in a room that offers endless views of the setting sun. After a solid sleep in crisp linens, make your way to your next destination. Be aware that the rooms are small and not able to house a family of four or more. We had two rooms with an adjoining door.

Fun fact: The piano that still sits in the hotel was carried up the mountain by six very strong men. Wow!

Hotel Weisshorn Details

Hotel Weisshorn
3961 St-Luc / info@weisshorn.ch / +41 27 475 11 06
www.weisshorn.ch / GPS: 46.20831, 7.61762

+ Small private rooms; towels and linens provided by the hotel
+ Shared bathrooms and showers
+ Heat is available in the rooms
+ Electricity and outlets in the rooms
+ Free Wi-Fi
+ Good cellular connectivity
+ Fixed menu. Vegetarian options available, request at the time of booking
+ Cash and credit cards accepted

Accommodation Overview for Cabane Bella-Tola

Bella-Tola is a perfectly located hut providing tremendous views. This basic, no-frills accommodation provides dormitory style rooms with a hearty evening meal.

Cabane Bella-Tola Details

Cabane Bella-Tola
3961 St-Luc / cabane@funiluc.ch / +41 27 476 15 67
cabanebellatola.ch / GPS: 46.23286, 7.61434

+ Modest, shared dormitory; sleep sacks and towels required
+ Shared bathrooms and showers
+ No heat in the rooms
+ Electricity and outlets in room
+ Free Wi-Fi
+ Moderate cellular connectivity
+ Fixed menu. Vegetarian options available, request at the time of booking
+ Cash and credit cards accepted

Kid Approved

+ The planet theme trail and its multiple installations.
+ The planetarium with the opportunity to look through a high-powered telescope.
+ The chocolate tortes and berry pie at Bella-Tola. So much chocolate and so many berries!
+ The Planet Park at Tignousa is a large playground that is a lot of fun for kids.

Tips

Tessa
Try to remember something you learned about the planets during dinner.

Parents
This tour can be completed in reverse making the first day easier, and perhaps lowering the trail difficulty to moderate instead of challenging.

Special Features

+ The planet theme trail is informational and educational
  for the entire family.
+ The planetarium of St-Luc. If you want to book special tours, request
  those tours in advance at: stationdesetoiles.ch
+ When you book your reservation online for Bella-Tola, they will email
  your receipt, which will include the QR code, granting access to the
  general area. This includes free admission to the planetarium.
+ This area (Val d'Anniviers) offers a free pass for lifts, buses and other
  activities in the area. Take advantage of this benefit, though only good
  for one day, from our experience. For more information visit:
  www.valdanniviers.ch
+ The views of the mountains and the Matterhorn.

Be Aware

+ Water and toilets are not available along the route.
+ The hike up to Hotel Weisshorn is steep and long. Plan accordingly.
+ During hot weather, pack plenty of water, sunscreen,
  hats and sunglasses.
+ Poles are recommended for this tour.
+ Bella-Tola is undergoing major renovations in 2021.
  Our description of the hut may change with the renovations.

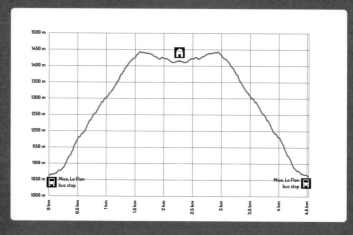

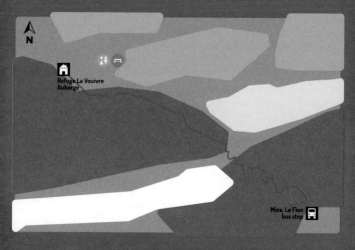

Picnic / Grilling

Toilet

Snakes,
No Ladders

START
Miex, Le Flon
(bus stop)

FINISH
Miex, Le Flon
(bus stop)

1415 m	4.6 km	425 m	425 m	1441 m	T1

2.3 km	1:45 h		2.3 km	1:25 h

Day 1

Day 2

390 m	35 m		35 m	390 m

Auberge
Refuge La Vouivre

Overview

Lac de Taney is a hidden gem. A small hamlet tucked away in a majestic setting and a location that should certainly be on your list to visit. What makes this area all the more special is the amount of work those insignificant 2.3 km will take you to reach your destination. The route is an uphill climb, with plenty of loose rocks to navigate, but do not allow that to deter you from making the trek.

Once you arrive at the lake, all the memories of the climb will quickly dissipate. The lake is a tranquil sanctuary set in a little nest of calm. We elected to stay two nights allowing our children the opportunity to play, explore and fall in love with the area. We felt remarkably relaxed upon our departure, which is the point of all of this.

Directions

Day 1
From the bus stop, Miex, Le Flon, proceed to the end of the parking lot. Make a sharp right up the trail, keeping left at the forks. The trail is not well marked, but is easy to follow. The trail continues to zig-zag and crosses a road after approximately 800 m. The zig-zag continues uphill for another 350 m before arriving at another road. The roads are all part of this route, so don't worry, you are going the right way! The road then crests after another 350 m, revealing expanding views of Lake Taney and the mountains surrounding it. Continue along the trail on your left, the Auberge Refuge La Vouivre will be on your right after 800 m.

Day 2
To return to Miex, Le Flon bus stop, follow the directions in reverse.

Trail Markers

Day 1
Le Flon ≫ Col de Taney ≫ Taney ≫ Auberge Refuge La Vouivre

Day 2
Auberge Refuge La Vouivre ≫ Taney ≫ Col de Taney ≫ Le Flon

Accommodation Overview

The auberge offers basic accommodations and tiny family rooms. The location is ideal if you want to take advantage of the lake, which is within walking distance from the *auberge*. Dinner can be enjoyed outside in good weather and breakfast is a simple affair.

Accommodation Details

Auberge Refuge La Vouivre
1896 Miex / +41 24 481 14 80
www.lactaney.com / GPS: 46.34507, 6.83257

+ Private family rooms available with sheets, duvets and towels
+ Shared bathroom and shower
+ Heat in the rooms
+ Electricity and outlets in the rooms
+ No Wi-Fi
+ Weak cellular connectivity
+ À la carte menu. Vegetarian options available
+ Cash and cards accepted, but not AMEX

Kid Approved

+ Your children will enjoy the lake.
+ The nature and wildlife are fantastic!

Tips

You will need to make a few stops along the way to play games (see chapter four) and take turns allowing the children to lead the walk. Please be prepared with lots of treats to keep motivation high and energy levels elevated. The trail is not marked particularly well, but if you are going up, you know you are on the right path.

Tessa
Look for snakes in the tall grass.

Parents
Try the *Tartiflette*, which is a potato, cheese, bacon, and onion casserole. It is remarkably delicious.

Special Features

+ The lake is in a lovely, peaceful setting.
+ The lake is ideal for swimming.
+ There are additional hiking opportunities in the area.
+ Grills are available at the lake.
+ There are toilets at the lake.
+ There is a dairy within walking distance from the hut, which sells yogurt, raclette, meringues, and other items.
+ Fishing is possible at the lake.

Be Aware

+ It is a tough uphill climb to the lake.
+ There are snakes in the area.
+ Pack a bathing suit for the lake and a small, quick-dry towel.
+ During the true height of summer, the area may be quite hot.
+ No water or food available along the trail up to the lake. Pack plenty of water and snacks.
+ Several rock fall areas are present on the way up to the lake. Proceed with caution.
+ The rocks will be slick when wet. Use caution and perhaps poles when hiking down.

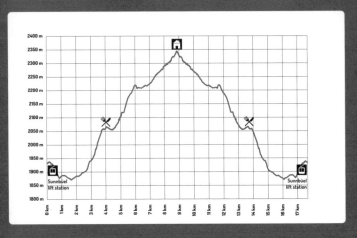

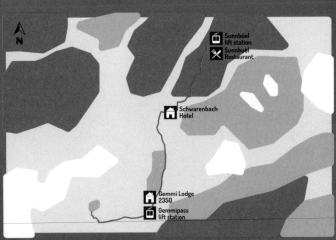

The Historic Gemmipass

START
Sunnbüel
(lift station)

FINISH
Sunnbüel
(lift station)

| 2350 m | 17.6 km | 670 m | 670 m | 2350 m | T1 |

8.8 km	4 h	8.8 km	3:40 h
Day 1		**Day 2**	
541 m	129 m	129 m	541 m

Gemmi Lodge 2350

Overview

The hike along Gemmipass is part of a famous trading route. Connecting two cantons, Bern and Valais, this pass has been used for centuries. The pass is along wide, open paths, making this route easy to navigate with children. The hike takes you along Daubensee and then ultimately on to the impressively situated Gemmi Lodge 2350. Hike up to the hotel, check in to your room and enjoy a coffee or drink in the lounge area, which offers remarkable views of the surrounding area and some famous Swiss peaks. On a clear day, the Matterhorn is visible.

If you happen to fall in love with the area – which honestly, isn't hard to do – consider extending this into a tour with a stay at Lämmerenhütte SAC, 2,503 m. Alternatively, take a hike to Lämmerensee (roughly 6 km roundtrip with an additional two hours) before heading out on the second day; the area looks like a moonscape, but with fresh air!

Directions

Day 1
Exit the Sunnbüel lift station, turning left following signs to Gemmipass. The trail will meander through pastures along a wide mountain road. After 2 km, there will be a farm on the right (Alpwirtschaft Spittelmatte) where you can buy alpine cheese. Behind this farm, down the path to the left, is a small gem of a lake, Arveseeli, which is shallow and quite picturesque. Continue along the main trail as this route is shorter and proceed to Gemmipass. The trail climbs, switches back, and progresses around a changing landscape of gray rock. Schwarenbach Berghotel is just around the corner, and is an ideal place to stop for a meal or if poor weather occurs during the hike. The trail continues up and through a narrower mountain section; however, the path remains quite wide. Above this section, the trail will level off and arrive at the lake, Daubensee. It is approximately another 2.8 km past the lake to Gemmi Lodge 2350.

Day 2
To head back to Sunnbüel, follow the directions in reverse or make the short walk to the Gemmibahn cable car to make your way easily down the mountain to Leukerbad.

Trail Markers

Day 1
Sunnbüel ≫ Spittelmatte ≫ Schwarenbach ≫ Gemmipass (Gemmi Lodge 2350)

Day 2
Gemmipass (Gemmi Lodge 2350) ≫ Schwarenbach ≫ Spittelmatte ≫ Sunnbüel

Accommodation Overview

Positioned on a striking cliff, this modern mountain hotel is a pretty remarkable place to spend the night. The glassed-in lounge encourages visitors to absorb the breathtaking views. Pull up a beanbag or a chair and relish in the beauty. This restaurant doesn't just serve delicious meals, but also delivers some delightful views as well. It is important to note that the water at the mountain hotel is not suitable for drinking, as the microbe levels are too high. The hotel offers tea to fill water bottles at breakfast for all hikers to take free of charge.

Acommondation Details

Gemmi Lodge 2350
3954 Leukerbad / +41 27 470 12 01
www.gemmi.ch / GPS: 46.39773, 7.61562

+ Private rooms available with sheets, duvets and towels
+ Shared bathrooms and showers
+ Heat is available in the rooms
+ Electricity and outlets in the rooms
+ Free Wi-Fi
+ Weak cellular connectivity
+ Fixed menu. Vegetarian options available, request at the time of booking
+ Cash and credit cards accepted

For those interested in extending the tour consider an overnight at either the Berghotel Schwarenbach or the Lämmerenhütte SAC.

Berghotel Schwarenbach
info@schwarenbach.ch / www.schwarenbach.ch / +41 33 675 12 72

Lämmerenhütte SAC
info@laemmerenhuette.ch / laemmerenhuette.ch / +41 27 470 25 15

Kid Approved

+ Animal spotting opportunities along the route,
  including sheep, cow and salamanders.
+ The two scenic lakes of Daubensee and Lämmerensee.
+ The hut is located in a pretty cool location. The massive windows with incredible views, plus overstuffed beanbags, all provide a very relaxed vibe.

Tips

Tessa
Stay together as a family.

Noah
Having truly waterproof gear is helpful when it rains.

Parents
Stop at Berghotel Schwarenbach for lunch or a snack, as this is the mid-way point. The hut dates back to 1742 and was home to some famous guests, including Pablo Picasso and Mark Twain. How cool is that? Don't forget to read up on or ask the innkeepers to tell you about the famous cat that once lived at the hotel. Such an extraordinary story!

Special Features

+ Wide, easy to navigate path with a gradual ascent/descent.
+ There is a sheep festival each year at Daubensee on the last Sunday in July, which must be an incredible sight to see. For more information visit: www.gemmi.ch
+ Access to the Gemmibahn (cable car) is free for overnight guests, taking you to Leukerbad.
+ There is an advanced *via ferrata* (Italian for "iron path," which consists of secured climbing routes up a mountain) just below the Gemmi Lodge 2350. This is not recommended to complete with children; however, it is impressive to witness climbers making their way up the route.
+ The portion of the hike in Valais is within the Pfyn-Finges Nature Park.
+ The lifts at both Sunnbüel and Gemmipass accept the *Halbtax* and the Junior Card. For more information visit: www.sunnbuel.ch and www.gemmi.ch

Be Aware

+ There are no toilets along the route until Berghotel Schwarenbach and again at Gemmi Lodge 2350.
+ Watch for salamanders if the trail is wet.
+ The water from the tap at Gemmi Lodge 2350 is not suitable for drinking.
+ The hike is above treeline; therefore, no shelter is available to protect you from the elements.
+ Despite the hotel being open in winter, this might be too difficult to navigate with children during this time.
+ It is not advisable to hike the pass down to Leukerbad with children.

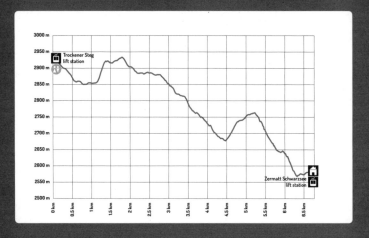

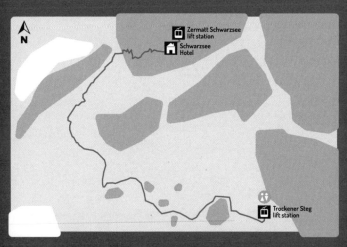

Toilet

VS
HOTEL SCHWARZSEE

Zermatt
Glacier Trail

25

START
Trockener Steg
(lift station)

FINISH
Zermatt Schwarzsee
(lift station)

2583 m	6.5 km	197 m	541 m	2929 m	T2

6.3 km	5 h
Day 1	
197 m	541 m

0.2 km	0:05 h
Day 2	
– –	– –

Hotel
Schwarzsee

Overview

If you are looking for an awe-inspiring, absolutely knock-your-socks-off type of hike search no further. The Zermatt Glacier trail places the Matterhorn in full view (on a clear day) for the duration of this route, making this hike dramatic throughout.

As you step off the gondola at the Trockener Steg lift station, you will feel as though you have been dropped off on another planet. Take some time to truly absorb the splendor that surrounds you. Thank your lucky stars we are no longer in the era of film and that digital cameras have now taken over, allowing you to capture hundreds of remarkable images without needing all of those rolls of film. The Matterhorn will be your guiding beacon throughout this hike.

Once at Hotel Schwarzsee, drop off your pack, and head outside to see if the Black Nose sheep are grazing in the area. These sheep are adorable and very friendly. Don't miss the sunset to end this perfect day!

Directions

Day 1
Exit the lift station and follow the path to the right and down to the small lake, Theo-dulgletschersee, which will not be immediately visible. You will see signs for the Matterhorn Glacier Trail. This trail is rather simple as there are no other trails in this area until Hirli (at 5 km), but it may become difficult to see the trail markers once the trail begins to descend. This is due to the color changes of the rock from gray to red-brown that will blend with the trail blazes. From Hirli, take the trail down to Schwarzsee and on to Hotel Schwarzsee.

Day 2
Take the lift down from Zermatt Schwarzsee (lift station).

Trail Markers

Day 1
Trockener Steg ≫ Hirli ≫ Schwarzsee

Day 2
Schwarzsee (Lift station)

Accommodation Overview

This hotel provides the perfect overnight stay after a long day on the trail. The hotel's terrace encourages you to have a drink and marvel at the view of the Matterhorn, making it the ideal spot to kick off your boots. The rooms are clean and welcoming. Wake up to the Matterhorn and a rich breakfast buffet, providing the perfect opportunity to fuel up before setting out.

You could extend this into a tour by staying a second night at the Schönbielhütte SAC, though this may be too far (9 km) for younger children. For more informatin visit www.schoenbielhuette.ch

Acommondation Details

Hotel Schwarzsee

3920 Zermatt / info@schwarzsee-zermatt.ch / +41 27 967 22 63
www.schwarzsee-zermatt.ch / GPS: 45.99158, 7.70944

+ Private rooms available with sheets, duvets and towels
+ Shared bathrooms and showers
+ Heat in the rooms
+ Electricity and outlets in the rooms
+ No Wi-Fi
+ Moderate cellular connectivity
+ Fixed menu. Vegetarian options available, request at the time of booking
+ Cash and credit cards accepted

Kid Approved

+ There are crystals and cool rocks to be discovered near the small lake
  by the Trockener Steg lift station, Theodulgletschersee.
+ The multiple lakes along the hike.
+ The Matterhorn, which will tower impressively over tiny bodies. With binoculars,
  ask your children if they can spot the Hörnlihütte located on the right-hand-side of
  the Matterhorn when facing the mountain. Whew ... what an impressive sight! This
  hut is the starting point for climbers daring to summit the Matterhorn on
  the Hörnli and Zmutt ridge. Those are some brave souls.
+ The resident Black Nose sheep that may make appearances at the *Berghotel*.
  Too cute for words.

Tips

Tessa
Look all over the first lake for crystals and garnets in the rocks.

Noah
Use the toilet before you hit the trail!

Parents
If you plan to stay in Zermatt, we would highly recommend the simple loop hike from Furi to the Dossen Glacier Garden. This route is packed with family fun activities and accessible from May through October. Cross the suspension foot bridge, visit the entertaining playground and hike through the Dossen Glacier Garden to gain valuable insight on the Gorner glacier. Make your way down the mountain back to Furi. Caution! Check lift operating times before you start your journey.

Special Features

+ The Matterhorn Glacier Trail is a theme trail with 23 information boards educating you about glaciers. The information panels are available in English, German, French and Japanese.
+ This hike is visually stunning throughout, especially on a clear day when the Matterhorn is view. Wow!
+ This hike provides the opportunity to educate your family on glaciers and climate change.
+ The lifts in Zermatt accept *Halbtax* and the Junior Card. For more information visit: www.zermatt.ch

Be Aware

+ There are no toilets or water facilities along this route. Plan accordingly.
+ This route is above treeline, therefore, there is no protection from the elements. Don't forget your hats, sunglasses and sunscreen.
+ Don't forget your camera!
+ From Hirli down to Schwarzsee, the trail narrows with switchbacks. Keep children on the inside of the trail.
+ The hotel is open in the winter, but we do not advise this route during the winter months.
+ The lift ticket kiosks may not offer the same tickets as a staffed counter would, for example the Junior Card discount. Pay attention to the options, there are no reimbursements once tickets have been purchased.

J F M A M J J A S O N D

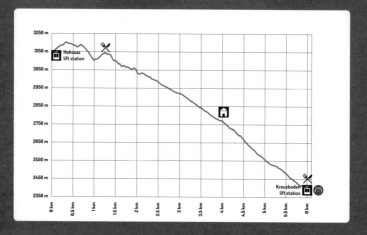

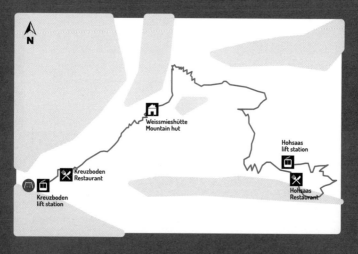

🎠 Playground

A Window
to the Peaks

START
Hohsaas
(lift station)

FINISH
Kreuzboden
(lift station)

2726 m	5.7 km	125 m	845 m	3200 m	T2

Day 1		Day 2	
3.9 km	3:20 h	1.8 km	1:40 h
118 m	513 m	7 m	322 m

Weissmieshütte
SAC

Overview

For a true alpine experience, immerse yourself in an area rich with peaks, glaciers, and expansive views. This high elevation hike and overnight is sure to provide you with a glimpse of what it is like for those who venture further into the mountains. Those adventurers depart in the early hours to reach some of the summits you will see on the "4,000 meter" path loop at Hohsaas. This loop, "Rundweg 18 Viertausender," will reveal some of the highest peaks in Switzerland. This walk leads you past the Trift Glacier. This short loop is marked with points of information about the peaks and the nature you will find at this elevation. Two small lakes and the view over the glacier are the perfect spot for a relaxing picnic. Look closely above the glacier, can you see the climbers coming off the ridge?

In the morning, enjoy a casual walk down to Kreuzboden looking for marmots and blueberries among the changing foliage in the autumn. Let the children play at the sprawling playground and enjoy a coffee at the restaurant at Kreuzboden.

Directions

Day 1
From Hohsaas, follow trail markers for the "Rundweg 18 Viertausender," which will start on the left, up the hill and behind the lift. This short loop concludes at the Panorama Restaurant, while the path to Weissmieshütte turns left down the hill under the lift station. The trail continues down through areas where glaciers once stood, now marked by desolate terrain and smooth rock. The Weissmieshütte is below a series of descending zig-zags.

Day 2
Kreuzboden is an almost straight descent. About midway, you may see marmots in the field on your left. The trail ends at the playground, which is just across from the lift and the restaurant at Kreuzboden.

Trail Markers

Day 1
Hohsaas >> (Rundweg 18 Viertausender) >> Weissmieshütte SAC

Day 2
Weissmieshütte SAC >> Kreuzboden

Accommodation Overview

Weissmieshütte is ideally situated with access to impressive peaks and serves as a starting point to reach the summits. Many climbers will depart in the early hours to reach them. A visit to Weissmieshütte is a window into the climbing world. The hut was created in 1894, which at the time, without access to lifts or helicopter support, was an enormous undertaking. The hut has undergone many revisions from its time of opening and has now been modernized, however, the original building still services overnight guests.

Acommondation Details

Weissmieshütte SAC
3910 Saas-Grund / huette@weissmieshuette.ch / +41 27 957 25 54
www.weissmieshuette.ch / GPS: 46.14374, 7.9779

+ Dormitories only; sleep sacks required
+ Shared bathrooms; no showers
+ Electricity, but no outlets in the room
+ No Wi-Fi
+ Good cellular connectivity
+ Fixed menu. Vegetarian options available, request at the time of booking
+ Cash and credit cards accepted

Kid Approved

+ The incredible playground and grilling area at Kreuzboden is worthy of hours of play and exploration.

Tip

Go in September, when the trails are less crowded. On your way down to Kreuzboden, the red bushes (just off the trail) are wild blueberries. If you want to enjoy more from this area, a hike from Mattmark to Monto Moro (Italian border) will also impress; it is an out-and-back hike just over 13 km with ibex grazing at the Tälliboden upper grassland in late August/September!

Special Features

+ Peak and glacier views are plentiful along the route.
+ The start of this trail takes you on the "Rundweg 18 Viertausender" loop,
  with incredible views of some of the highest peaks in Switzerland.
+ Wide open and expansive views are visible throughout!
+ This area provides a genuine feeling for the Alps.

Be Aware

+ The primary purpose of the hut is to house climbers
  who will rise early to reach summits in the area.
+ The elevation exceeds 3,000 m and may cause some to have
  headaches or dizziness, so drink plenty of water
  and take your time on the hike.
+ The lift from Sass-Grund accepts *Halbtax* and Junior Cards,
  for more information visit www.saas-fee.ch
+ The time to the hut depends on how long you stay at the lakes,
  the glacier, and/or the Panorama Restaurant.
+ Toilets are located at the lift stations, restaurants and the hut.
+ The hut is open in winter, but we do not recommend this route with
  children during the winter season.

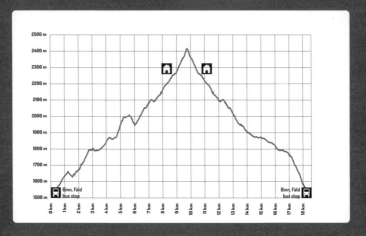

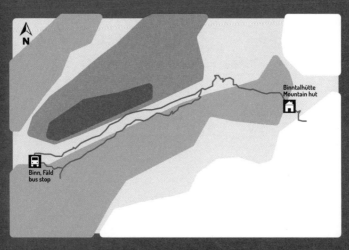

The Crystal Valley

27

START
Binn, Fäld
(bus stop)

FINISH
Binn, Fäld
(bus stop)

2275 m	15.8 km	919 m	919 m	2409 m	T2

8.4 km	4:10 h		7.4 km	2:50 h
Day 1			**Day 2**	
891 m	136 m		28 m	783 m

Binntalhütte
SAC

Overview

The Binn Valley is one of the richest mineral areas in Switzerland and the Langenbach quarry ranks as one of the top ten most diverse mineral locations in the world. In fact, some varieties of crystals are only found at this site. A hike to the Binntal hut is perhaps best enjoyed over several nights, to experience the pure remoteness of the area. This peaceful region is just a short distance from the Albrun Pass, which leads into Italy. Stop at the Lengenbach quarry, a short 1.5 km into the hike, and encourage your children to search for tiny, colorful crystals hidden within the white dolomite rock. If you are looking for larger quartz crystals, a good eye is needed. Keep an eye out for needle quartz in streams or in the grassy areas at higher elevations near the hut. But don't just gaze down, as the geology is present in the spectacular mountains too. On a clear night, step outside and look to the heavens, the crystals are surely reflected there, offering amazing views of the countless stars!

Directions

Day 1
From the Fäld bus stop, walk up the road passing the Café Imfeld on your left. After approximately 800 m, you will see a sign for the "Mineraliengrube Langenbach;" the 700 m deviation is worth taking the time to discover with children. Once back on the trail, continue past the waypoint "Figgerscha" toward "Binntalhütte SAC." After 4.2 km, the trail splits, continue left in the direction of Binntalhütte by crossing the river, then keeping right, and connecting with the gravel road up the hill. Note: At this point where the trail splits, you can keep right and opt to hike up to Halsensee (lake), this will add approximately 30 minutes or more to your overall hiking time. If coming from the lake, the trail will descend and cross the river. Turn right and continue up the grassy hill mixed with white exposed dirt. The trail will continue to zig-zag up for another 1 km before leveling out at the waypoint "Blatt." This area is a flat, wet upper pasture, where the trail meanders up to the hut an additional 1.6 km ahead. An optional trip to the Swiss-Italian border at the Albrun Pass is less than 1 km away, and gains 140 m.

Day 2
To return to Fäld, walk the directions in reverse, but continue following the trail down the gravel road from Wiissbach. Watch for cars along the road, as the trail remains on this road and crosses it on your way down. Once in Fäld, turn left onto the road heading back to the bus stop.

Trail Markers

Day 1
Fäld >> Figgerscha >> Halsensee >> Blatt >> Binntalhütte >> Albrunpass (optional) >> Binntalhütte

Day 2
Binntalhütte >> Wiissbach >> Freichi >> Trogschluecht >> Fäld

Accommodation Overview

The Binntalhütte was originally built as a military observation post during World War II, as it stands less than one kilometer from the Italian border. It has been damaged by avalanches several times over the years; the most recent being in 1989 and again in 2017. Since then, it has been beautifully renovated and prides itself on its low environmental impact.

Acommondation Details

Binntalhütte SAC
3996 Binn / +41 27 971 47 97
www.cabane-binntal.ch / GPS: 46.3747, 8.29187

+ Dormitories only; sleep sacks required
+ Shared bathrooms; no showers
+ No heat in the rooms
+ Electricity, but no outlets in the room
+ No Wi-Fi
+ Weak cellular connectivity
+ Fixed menu. Vegetarian options available, request at the time of booking
+ Carry trash out with you
+ Cash only accepted

Kid Approved

Crystals ... so many crystals!

Tip

Bring an eye loop/magnifying glass to view the crystals, as many are small but look amazing with magnification. Crystals may not be visible on the trail, however, should you elect to veer off the trail in search of crystals, do so with caution and care.

Special Features

+ This is one of the most diverse mineral areas in the world.
+ The area is remote and in a very quiet setting.
+ Part of the trail is along the Rock Adventure Trail
  (Gesteins-Erlebnisweg).
+ A visit to the Mineral Museum of André Gorsatt will surely impress
  and show some of the best examples of minerals in the area:
  www.andre-gorsatt.ch
+ The hut can provide a packed lunch for a small fee.

Be Aware

+ This is a nature park; be respectful while exploring the area.
+ Some digging areas are private and digging may require a permit; it is
  possible to hire a guide who knows the valley and locations
  of crystals. For more information visit www.landschaftspark-binntal.ch
+ A toilet is located at the start of the hike,
  at the bus stop and at Binntalhütte.
+ Carry out all of your trash and do not leave it at the hut.
  This minimizes the environmental impact on Binntalhütte.
+ Parking is available at the Fäld bus stop area.
+ For more information about the Lengenbach Mineral digging area
  visit: www.grube-lengenbach.ch
+ Plan for a longer hiking time if you visit the Langenbach digging area
  or Halsensee lake, longer than 1 hour (combined)
  on the way to Binntalhütte.

J F M A M J J A S **O** N **D**

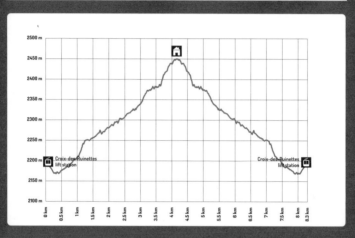

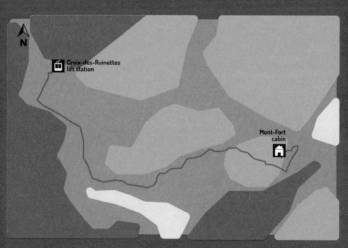

VS
CABANE MONT FORT CAS

High Above Verbier

START
Croix–des–Ruinettes
(lift station)

FINISH
Croix–des–Ruinettes
(lift station)

⌂ 2457 m	⊢ 8.2 km	↗ 313 m	↘ 313 m	⩕ 2457 m	T1

⊢ 4.1 km	⏱ 1:45 h	⊢ 4.1 km	⏱ 1:30 h
Day 1		**Day 2**	
↗ 285 m	↘ 28 m	↗ 28 m	↘ 285 m

Cabane Mont Fort
CAS

Overview

This pleasant hike starts in the pristine town of Verbier. Stroll through the town and get a pulse for the area before making your way to the lift station. Once off the lift, allow yourselves to be captivated by the lovely scenery. The children will take pleasure in walking along the *bisses*, which date back to the 13th century. These waterways are irrigation systems that deliver water to the surrounding areas. The Bisse de Levron was created in the mid 1400s.

As you continue your walk, you will notice Cabane Mont Fort in the distance. This hut is old with a rich history. Built in the year 1925, the cabin was constructed as a way to prosper from the mountains in the area. Its location is convenient for those participating in the "Haute Route," and after a renovation in 2001, the hut now welcomes hikers, skiers and families of all ages.

As you continue to make your way up to the hut, divert your attention to the surrounding mountains, which are superb. Drop your belongings in your room, wash-up before dinner and relax in the antique living room, but before doing so, walk out onto the terrace to relish in a brilliant sunset.

Directions

Day 1
Exit the lift station and turn right, heading downhill and toward Bisse de Levron/ Mont Fort. This will lead downhill approximately 250 m until you see a sign for Bisse de Levron on the left. After 500 m, use caution as mountain bikers will cross the trail. The trail will continue along Bisse de Levron for another 250 m; the trail to Cabane Mont Fort will deviate to the left and continue along Bisse Raye des Verbiérins. The trail will continue along this bisse for another 2 km until it turns left up toward Cabane Mont Fort approximately 500 m up the hill.

Day 2
For the return, follow the directions in reverse.

Trail Markers

Day 1
Les Ruinettes ➤➤ Mont Font

Day 2
Mont Font ➤➤ Les Ruinettes

Accommodation Overview

Cabane Mont Fort sits at the top of a mountain offering expansive views in every direction. This hut is attended to with great care, which is noticeable by the tiny vases filled with wildflowers placed lovingly on all the tables. The interior of the hut is rustic yet welcoming with warm wooden tones. The sleeping quarters are simple dormitory style rooms, offering a bed and shared bathroom facilities. As the evening meal is served, sink low into your chair, relax and reflect on your day.

Acommondation Details

Cabane Mont Fort CAS

1936 Verbier / cabanemontfort@verbier.ch / +41 27 778 13 84
www.cabanemontfort.com / GPS: 46.08352, 7.28104

+ Private, modest bunk bedrooms; sleep sacks required
+ Shared bathroom with a pay for shower; towels are required
+ No heat in the rooms
+ Electricity and outlet in the room
+ No Wi-Fi
+ Good cellular connectivity
+ À la carte meals – vegetarian options available
+ Carry trash out with you
+ Cash and credit cards accepted

Kid Approved

+ The Bisse de Levron and Bisse Raye des Verbiérins along the trail.
  Please never throw anything into a *bisse*.
+ The fact that the SAC hut allows you to order off the menu.
  The *Rösti* is delicious!

Tips

Noah
Look for interesting beetles and caterpillars along the trail.

Parents
Due to the high elevation of this hut, warm clothing is essential. Thicker sleeping bags help ensure warmth during your overnight stay, weather depending.

Special Features

+ The Bisse de Levron and the Bisse Raye des Verbiérins.
+ This hike doesn't require too much physical effort.
+ This area (Verbier) offers the VIP pass for people staying overnight
  in the area. Obtain your pass at the tourist office before arriving at
  the lift, this will allow free lift access for one day only, or equal to the
  number of nights you are staying. The lift does not accept *Halbtax* or
  Junior Cards. For more information, visit: www.verbier.ch

Be Aware

+ The hut may be cold, depending upon the weather
  and the season of your visit.
+ The hut is located on a cliff, please watch children carefully.
+ Some of the hiking trails are shared with bikers. Please be respectful
  and use caution when hiking.
+ For those electing to drive, a parking lot is located on the opposite
  side of the town, located near the sports center. Should you park at
  that location, it will add another 3 km roundtrip to your total distance.

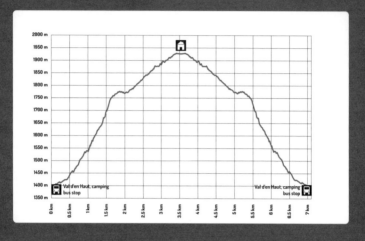

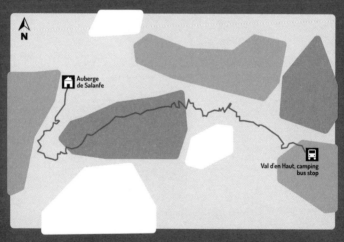

VS

AUBERGE DE SALANFE

The Top of the Dam

29

START	FINISH
Van-d'en-Haut, camping *(bus stop)*	**Van-d'en-Haut, camping** *(bus stop)*

1940 m	6.8 km	571 m	571 m	1940 m	T2

Day 1

3.4 km	2 h	554 m	17 m

Day 2

3.4 km	1:30 h	17 m	544 m

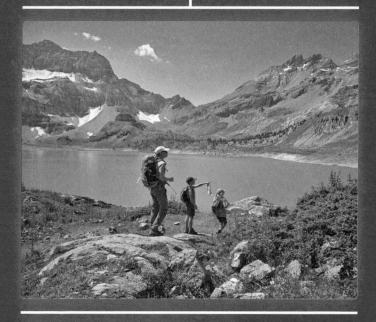

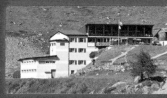

Auberge de Salanfe

Overview

Prepare to climb for this hike, however, know that the duration is short and the reward is grand. There is a famous quote by Theodore Roosevelt, the 26th president of the U.S. that reads, "Believe you can and you're halfway there." Remind yourself of that quote as you climb up to Auberge de Salanfe. As you eventually get closer to the auberge, stop at the small creek to soak your feet before the final ascent. This will make the children giggle and you smile. Once at the auberge, pull up a chair facing the lake, remove your boots, and order a fresh slice of apricot cake. Now it's time to relax because you made it. Good for you!

Check into your room or dormitory and if you still have energy remaining, consider a slow stroll around the lake, which is roughly 5 km. The wild flowers are abundant, the views are photo worthy and the cows might just greet you as you pass. Moments and locations such as this are the reason why we hike.

Enjoy your evening meal in the communal dining room. Before you fall asleep, make sure you move outside to admire the stars and the moon reflecting off of the lake. It's magical up there for sure!

Directions

Day 1
From the Van d'en Haut, camping bus stop, proceed uphill toward Salanfe. If you drive, the parking for Salanfe is past the camping area across a bridge and up the hill. The trail will begin on the edge of the parking area and will connect with the main trail. By driving, you will shorten the total length by approximately 1.2 km. The trail will soon arrive at a series of switchbacks with steps. We named this section of the trail "the 500 steps;" how many do you count? Although the trail is short, it is quite steep for the first 1.5 km before it begins to level off. The dam will become visible in the next 500 m as the trail straightens. The trail will continue up, though not as steep, and will veer right toward the top of the dam. The auberge will be on the right side of the dam.

Day 2
Follow the directions in reverse for the return.

Trail Markers

Day 1
Van d'en Haut >> Salanfe

Day 2
Salanfe >> Van d'en Haut

Accommodation Overview

Auberge de Salanfe sits snuggly between the Trient and Dents du Midi peaks. This is a remarkable location in a world of serene surroundings. This area encourages you to breathe deeply and slow down. With the outdoor terrace, delicious food and pleasant innkeepers, your stay is certain to be memorable. The private family rooms are clean and the views from the rooms are pretty sweet too!

Acommodation Details

Auberge de Salanfe
1922 Salvan / auberge@salanfe.ch / +41 27 761 14 38
www.salanfe.ch / GPS: 46.14455, 6.97065

+ Private family rooms available with sheets, duvets and towels
+ Sleep sacks required for the dormitory
+ Shared shower and bathrooms
+ Heat and a sink in the rooms
+ Electricity and outlets in the room
+ No Wi-Fi
+ Good cellular connectivity
+ Fixed menu. Vegetarian options available, request at the time of booking
+ Cash and credit cards accepted

Kid Approved

+ The swings and freedom to roam once at the hut.
+ The apricot cake because it's always about the cake!

Tip

Try the Seven Peaks beer at the hut. We were big fans of the Cathédrale brew. Delicious!

Special Features

+ This exceptional area includes the Salanfe Dam, which was constructed from 1947–1952. There are plaques in the area that describe the construction and history.
+ Walking around the lake to truly absorb all the views is advised.
+ There is an old gold and arsenic mine just above Les Ottans with some remains of the infrastructure from the 1920s for those interested in a side trip. This is approximately 6.4 km from the auberge, or will add an additional 3 km to the loop around the lake.
+ This is not an overly populated area and void of tourists.
+ The hut will kindly pack you a picnic lunch for the next day; however, place your order during the evening meal. Pick-up your packed lunch upon departure.
+ The area of Salanfe is in-between four different tours of Dents Blanches, du Ruan, Dents du Midi, and Vallée du Trient. For more information visit: www.tour-dentsblanches.com, www.tourduruan.com, www.dentsdumidi.ch, www.valleedutrient.ch
+ The geology above the lake exhibits layers from the last 400 million years.
+ The hut sells fishing licenses for the well-stocked lake.

Be Aware

+ Poles are advised for this route, however, be aware that the route has exposed roots and rocks.
+ There is a section with lots of steep stairs to navigate. Please assist your little people on this portion of the hike.
+ Use extra caution if the route is wet, which will cause the path and the stairs to be quite slippery.
+ Watch children closely as they walk over the dam.
+ There are no water filling stations or toilets along the route. Pack plenty of water.

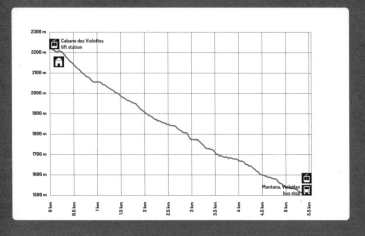

2300 m
2200 m — Cabane des Violettes lift station
2100 m
2000 m
1900 m
1800 m
1700 m
1600 m — Montana, Violettes bus stop
1500 m

0 km 0.5 km 1 km 1.5 km 2 km 2.5 km 3 km 3.5 km 4 km 4.5 km 5 km 5.5 km

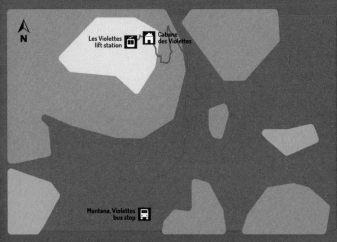

N

Les Violettes lift station   Cabane des Violettes

Montana, Violettes bus stop

VS
CABANE DES VIOLETTES CAS

High Above
Crans-Montana

30

START
Cabane–des–Violettes
(lift station)

FINISH
Montana, Violettes
(bus stop)

| 2208 m | 5.6 km | 36 m | 750 m | 2220 m | T1 |

150 m	0:05 h		5.6 km	2:30 h
Day 1			**Day 2**	
--	--		36 m	750 m

Cabane des Violettes
CAS

Overview

Crans-Montana is a true haven for families. We would recommend you get a genuine feel for the area before making your way up the mountain. Keep in mind, you will be hiking the second day of this excursion. The first day is designed for exploration. Consider stopping in the main town of Montana; take a leisurely stroll around Lake Grenon before you arrive at a little park. There is a dwarf theme trail around the lake, which is free, offering little stories as you walk around. Pick-up provisions for a picnic and benefit from this family-friendly area.

Upon your arrival at the hut, you will notice it is hovering on the edge of a mountain, offering breathtaking views of the layered mountains in the distance. As the cowbells ring and the sun sets, relax on the terrace and watch as the magic unfolds. When you rise in the morning, eat your breakfast and make your way down the mountain. The views will continue to impress and once you pick-up the Bisse du Tsittoret, the children will appreciate the opportunity to search for frogs along the route. The water has a calming effect on you as you drop in elevation.

Directions

Day 1
Cabane des Violettes will be visible from the gondola, on the right, in the direction of travel, as you approach the Les Violettes lift station. Exit the lift station and proceed to Cabane des Violettes.

Day 2
On the second day, walk toward the lift station; however, turn right at the Les Violettes trail marker sign post heading in the direction of Colombire/Plumachit. The trail will descend, switching back several times for approximately 2.2 km and cross a large stream. The trail will fork at the Bisse de Tsittoret. Turn left here and continue to descend toward Montana/Crans along the *bisse*. Continue following Bisse de Tsittoret in the direction of Les Barzettes and down to the Montana, Violettes bus stop.

Trail Markers

Day 1
Les Violettes

Day 2
Les Violettes ≫ Bisse du Tsittoret ≫ Les Barzettes

Accommodation Overview

Cabane des Violettes is perfectly positioned above the treeline on the edge of a small cliff. This offers superior views of the entire area. This rustic, yet cozy hut provides good meals and a terrace with a trendy vibe. The rooms and bathrooms are simple and the evening meal is a delicious experience.

Acommondation Details

Cabane des Violettes CAS

3963 Crans-Montana / info@cabanedesviolettes.ch / +41 27 481 39 19
www.cabanedesviolettes.ch / GPS: 46.34237, 7.50005

+ Private family rooms and dormitories available; sleep sacks required
+ Shared bathrooms with shower, towel required
+ Heat in the rooms
+ Electricity and outlets in the rooms
+ No Wi-Fi
+ Good cellular connectivity
+ Fixed menu. Vegetarian options available, request at the time of booking
+ It is not advised to drink the water at the hut. Purchase water at the hut for the hike down the mountain
+ Cash or credit cards accepted

Kid Approved

+ There are two fun swings at the hut.
+ The walk down from the hut along the *bisse* is quite relaxing.
+ If the hut serves fondue during your visit, enjoy that delicious experience.

Tips

Tessa
Look for frogs in and around the Bisse du Tsittoret.

Parents
Try the homemade pine bud schnapps at the hut. The chef makes it from local pine trees and though it is sweet, it is delicious and particularly good after fondue. Yum!

Special Features

+ Keep an eye open (while on the lift) for the chamois on the craggy cliffs approximately 350 m from the Les Violettes lift station.
+ This route has easy access made possible by the gondola. Always check the operating times of the gondola. For more information visit: www.mycma.ch
+ This is a relatively downhill, easy route along the Bisse du Tsittoret.
+ The Marmot Trail, starting at Cry-d'Er lift station passes the Les Violettes lift station and Cabane des Violettes. Starting the hike from Cry-d'Er will add approximately 2.3 km to this route.

Be Aware

+ This route is not recommended during heavy rain as the *bisse* may overflow causing washout on the trail.
+ There is no drinking water available along the route.
+ There are toilets at the lift stations and the hut.
+ Poles are recommended for this hike.
+ Access to the hut is dependent on lift operating times. Always check before starting your journey.

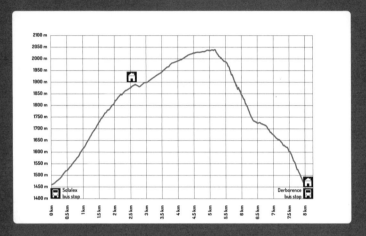

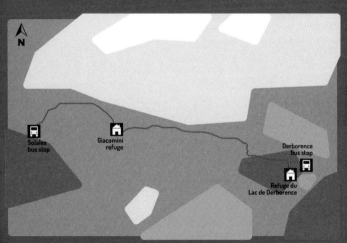

VD / VS

REFUGE GIACOMINI / REFUGE DU LAC DE DERBORENCE

Accessing
the Wild

START	FINISH
Solalex	**Derborence**
(bus stop)	*(bus stop)*

🏠	⊢⊣	↗	↘	⩓	🎚
1893 m	8.3 km	633 m	626 m	2038 m	T2
1480 m					

⊢⊣ 2.7 km	🕐 1:50 h	⊢⊣ 5.4 km	🕐 4 h	⊢⊣ 0.2 km	🕐 0:05 h
Day 1		**Day 2**		**Day 3**	
↗ 439 m	↘ 7 m	↗ 194 m	↘ 619 m	↗ ––	↘ ––

 Refuge
Giacomini

 Refuge
du Lac de Derborence

Overview

This two-day tour allows you to enjoy remote and pure nature at its finest. This is one area that still feels relatively wild, which makes it all the more alluring. The slow and gradual climb to Refuge Giacomini is a truly pleasurable experience for the senses. On several occasions we stopped to appreciate the views and took the opportunity to spot ibex high on the mountainside. Don't forget your binoculars!

Upon arrival at the Refuge Giacomini, located in the Anzeindaz mountain meadow, a peaceful overnight stay awaits. Nature in the area is largely untouched, as it is positioned in a wildlife area that is protected. Void of mass tourism; this hut is insulated from modern day distractions.

The second day, make your way slowly to Refuge du Lac de Derborence. The first portion of the hike is on wide-open trails, which allows your children the freedom to run and roam as they wish. As parents, we love this type of trail. You will be surrounded by pristine nature as you make your way down the mountain, where the paths narrow and descend. Once at your second overnight stay, drop off your bags in your room and head out to explore the lake.

Directions

Day 1
The bus will drop you off in the parking lot in front of the Grand Muveran information board. The trail begins through the gate at Solalex, on the left when facing the information board. Follow the trail uphill toward Anzeinde/Derborence. The names Anzeinde and Anzeindaz are synonymous along this trail. The trail will soon leave the mountain road and take you through a forest, uphill, and across a few sections that appear to be washed out from heavy rain. The trail leads to a farm area with several buildings. Refuge Giacomini will be visible a short way up the hill past the trail intersection.

Day 2
Begin by turning right at the intersection (when your back is toward Refuge Giacomini). This will take you up the hill toward Derborence through a broad field. Use caution through the field, particularly when calves are present, as you hike among the cows. The trail may be hard to find at times among the cow paths. A keen eye will see the matted grass from other walkers, but in any case, walk toward the low point in the crest of the mountain ahead. You will see two enormous boulders marked with trail blazes. Continue along to Pas de Cheville and descend toward Derborence. The trail is simple to follow once in the forest, and will turn right leading to Deborence. The Refuge du Lac de Derborence is at the bottom of the trail just above the lake.

Day 3
Departure. Keep track of the time; the bus only stops twice a day, so you must be prepared and know the time table! The bus stop is roughly 250 m down the trail on your left, when facing the lake.

Trail Markers

Day 1
Solalex » Anzeindaz (Refuge Giacomini)

Day 2
Anzeindaz (Refuge Giacomini) » Pas de Cheville » Derborence

Day 3
Derborence

Accommodation Overview
for Refuge Giacomini

This Refuge is charming and handled with care. The rooms are sweet and cozy and provide everything you need for a relaxing overnight stay. Our room offered a lovely skylight, providing a stunning view of the night sky. The shared bathrooms are located down the hall from the rooms.

Refuge Giacomini Details

Refuge Giacomini
1882 Gryon / refuge@anzeindaz.com / +41 24 498 22 95
www.anzeindaz.com / GPS: 46.2883, 7.16204

+ Private family rooms available with sheets, duvets and towels
+ Shared bathroom and shower
+ Heat in the rooms
+ Electricity and outlets in the rooms
+ No Wi-Fi
+ Weak cellular connectivity
+ Fixed menu. Vegetarian options available, book in advance
+ Cash and cards accepted

Accommodation Overview for Refuge du Lac de Derborence

This refuge rests in sight of the lake and offers its guests rooms with incredibly high bunk beds. This area is rich with history and was destroyed when the entire Southern section of the Diablerets massif collapsed in the year 1714 and again in 1749, which was devastating for the locals. The area has long since been rebuilt and is now a thriving region for hikers, bikers and nature lovers. To read more about the local area, check out C.F. Ramuz's book, *Deborence*, which was published in 1934 and later adapted into a film by Francis Reusser.

Refuge du Lac de Derborence Details

Refuge du Lac de Derborence
1976 Aven-Conthey / info@refugederborence.ch /
+41 27 346 14 28 / +41 79 449 46 87
www.refugederborence.ch / GPS: 46.27992, 7.21462

+ Private family rooms available with sheets and duvets
+ Bring your own towel
+ Shared bathrooms and showers
+ Electricity and outlets in the rooms
+ No Wi-Fi
+ Weak cellular connectivity
+ À la carte menu. Vegetarian options available.
+ Cash and cards accepted

Kid Approved

+ There is always something to discover along the trail: flowers, butterflies, beetles, and animals. Bring binoculars to spot ibex, chamois, and bearded vultures at Lac de Derborence.

Tip

After you have finished your evening meal at Refuge Giacomini, head outside to witness the sunset and the mesmerizing night sky. The area is perfect for safely walking around during the twilight hours. Encourage your children to look for nocturnal animals in the area. During our night walk, we saw a fox.

Special Features

+ Marvelous views throughout this tour.
+ Refuge Giacomini was established in 2009 and in 2019 they celebrated their 10th year of operation. Congratulations!
+ This tour provides the opportunity to disconnect and truly immerse your family in unspoiled nature.
+ This tour overlaps other impressive routes including: the Tour Des Muverans (www.tourdesmuverans.ch), a 54 km loop around the Grande Muveran, a mountain ridge divided between Vaud and Valais; the Tour de l'Argentine (www.villars-diablerets.ch), a 13 km loop around the l'Argentine mountain, the northwest smooth face can be seen on this hike from Solalex; and the famous through hike, the Via Alpina – red route (www.via-alpina.org), an intense 2600+ km / 161 stage hike from Trieste to Monaco!

Be Aware

+ No water or toilets on the trail, except at the start of the hike.
+ Several rock fall areas present along the route, proceed with caution.
+ You are above treeline; bring sunglasses, sunscreen and hats.
+ The area is very remote. Bring everything you need to get from one hut to the next.
+ The bus schedule departing Refuge du Lac de Derborence is extremely limited. View and plan your departure in advance. The bus trip down the mountain is a genuine experience. Hold on to your hats; this is one wild ride!

J F M A M J J A S O N D

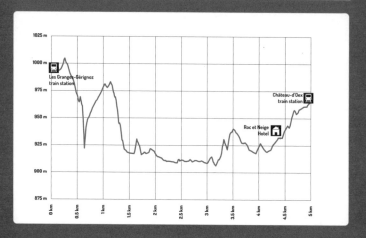

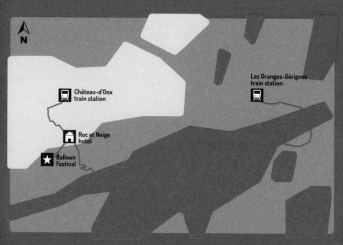

When Balloons Take Flight

32

START
Les Granges–Gérignoz
(train station)

FINISH
Château-d'Oex
(train station)

930 m	5 km	163 m	199 m	1003 m	T1

4.4 km	2:10 h		0.6 km	0:20 h
Day 1			**Day 2**	
163 m	199 m		––	––

Hotel
Roc et Neige

Overview

In the quaint town of Château-d'Oex, the annual International Hot Air Balloon Festival takes place for nine eventful days at the end of January. During this time, the town is transformed into a world of colorful balloons and activities. Observing the balloons with the snowy mountains in the backdrop is breathtaking.

The Hot Air Balloon Festival was created in 1979 and celebrates the world tour of Bertrand Piccard and Brian Jones in the Breitling Orbiter, which is on display in the town. With loads of activities, museums, events and even passenger flights, this is an event that is an enriching experience for your entire family. With an easy walk from Les Granges-Gérignoz train station, you will emerge from the forest to witness the sky filled with colorful balloons. Stay a weekend or a night, but pack the camera, some warm clothes and enjoy this magical experience.

While visiting this spectacular area, do not forget to visit Pays-D'Enhaut, which is known for the ancient tradition/art of paper cutting. A historic tradition that is alive and well in Vaud, with the local museum (Musée du Pays-d'Enhaut) that displays these gorgeous works of art, as well as informs visitors about daily life in the mountains. During the time of the International Hot Air Balloon Festival, you are invited into their workshops to observe this custom and witness the skills of the local artisans.

Directions

Day 1

At the Les Granges-Gérignoz train station, use caution as the train stops next to a road (Rue du Closalet). Follow signs to Gérignoz (not Château d'Oex). Walk down to the main road (Route de Saanen). Use caution crossing the road, turning left, and following the trail down along Route de Gérignoz. Use further caution when walking through the tunnel. Cross the bridge and take the third right (Seefeldweg), following signs to Château d'Oex via Pont Turrian, 1 h. The road (Seefeldweg) will curve right, and turn off the road after 500 m. Follow the trail down, this will lead you to and along the river (La Sarine) which is a nicer route. Continue, following signs to Pont Turrian which is the oldest suspension bridge in this area of Switzerland. The trail will zig-zag uphill, through a field, and to a road (Route des Monnaires). This road will merge onto another road of the same name. Ahead is the Hotel Roc & Neige, the small road to the left (Le Berceau) will lead to a field where the balloon festival takes place.

Day 2

For departing, make your way up the road (Route des Monnaires), using caution to cross the main road (Route de Saanen). Follow the trail markers uphill into the town. Continue on the narrow road (Ch. Des Ballons) and past the balloon capsule which travelled the world. Turn right onto Grand Rue. The Château d'Oex train station will be approximately 300 m ahead on your left.

Trail Markers

Day 1
Les Granges » Gérignoz » Château d'Oex

Day 2
Château d'Oex » Château d'Oex Gare

Accommodation Overview

This perfectly situated hotel allows you to fully partake in all of the hot air balloon activities, which are all within walking distance. You may even see the balloons in flight from your hotel room depending on the direction the wind blows. The rooms are simple with private bathrooms.

Acommodation Details

Hotel Roc & Neige

1660 Château-d'Oex / info@rocetneige.ch / +41 26 924 33 50
www.roc-et-neige.ch / GPS: 46.47166, 7.13277

+ Private family rooms available with sheets, duvets and towels
+ Heat in the rooms
+ Electricity and outlets in the rooms
+ Free Wi-Fi
+ Good cellular connectivity
+ Cash and credit cards accepted

Kid Approved

+ What kid doesn't love hot air balloons and stunt planes?
+ Watching the colorful balloons lift-off is truly a thrilling opportunity for children.

Tips

Though the Château d'Oex International Hot Air Balloon Festival takes place only once a year, it is important to know that the balloons do not fly when it snows. Have alternative plans in the event you hit the festival during a particularly snowy year.

Special Features

+ The International Hot Air Balloon Festival is truly a sight worth seeing. The event lasts a full week and offers an array of activities, including a children's day, an evening when the balloons are lit at night, passenger flights, and much, much more.
+ The hike/snowshoe adventure is an easy, beautiful route along a lovely river and is possible year-round.
+ Our hotel provided us with a small booklet entitled, *Pass D'Enhaut*, which provides discounted rates for museums, sports, the cinema, food and more.
+ To learn more about the Musée du Pays-d'Enhaut, please visit: www.musee-chateau-doex.ch

Be Aware

+ There is no toilet on the route, so have your group use the toilet on the train before getting off at the Les Granges-Gérignoz train station.
+ Water is not available on the route.
+ The trail may be icy during the winter months. We can highly recommend micro spikes for better grip on the ice.
+ The first few minutes of this route are slightly precarious. The trail leads you through a rock fall area, so proceed with caution, or walk through the car tunnel using the small sidewalk.
+ The hotel is located in the ideal spot for the Hot Air Balloon Festival, but reservations must be made far in advance.
+ The hotel did not offer dinner services while we visited because the chef was catering the festival. Check in advance with the hotel if you require an evening meal and book an alternative restaurant in the area. A nice alternative is the Le Chalet restaurant, which is a short walk from the hotel. For more information visit: www.lechalet-fromagerie.ch
+ A fee is required to enter the balloon area. For detailed information regarding the festival visit: www.festivaldeballons.ch

Fun Along the Way

> "
>
> Nature is a tool to get children to experience not just the wider world, but themselves.
>
> "
>
> STEPHEN MOSS
> ENGLISH NATURAL HISTORIAN, BIRDER AND AUTHOR

Parents   **Kids**

Chapter four was designed as a way to create fun and educational opportunities for your family as you hike through the gorgeous landscapes in Switzerland. We have provided activities to help you adventure longer and assist children in the learning process.

When the going gets rough, as it sometimes does when you journey long and far with children, simply refer to some of the activities outlined in this chapter. Regardless of the mood that infuses the group, know this: The time you spend as a family or with friends in the mountains is invaluable. Nature has a way of leveling us all, of creating life-long bonds and infusing memories that will last a lifetime. Our hope is that your family will reflect on your trail days with full hearts and a deep connection to the natural world, which is one of our most meaningful relationships.

A personal family favorite is to take turns asking questions on the trail, through the "Get to Know You" portion of this chapter. These questions are designed to get your group thinking and the ideas rolling. They also serve as a great distraction for the kilometers you cover and the mountains you will climb.

Some of the activities are designed for children to complete independently (labeled with the "kids" icon), while other activities require the assistance, initiation, or equipment from the adults in the group (labeled with the "parents" icon).

We are indebted to our readers for adventuring with us and our hope is that you continue to step into nature as a family for years to come. Now, go lace up those boots and get going. Beautiful adventures are waiting for you!

Conversation Starters on the Trail

As the kilometers stretch on, spark meaningful conversation with these fun and engaging questions. Each question can be asked by adults to children or children to adults.

+ Would you prefer to go back in time or ahead to the future? Why?
+ What does honesty mean to you? Is it ever okay to tell a lie?
+ What is one thing you can do each day to make the world a better place?
+ If you had ten million francs, but had to use your money to better the world, how would you spend your money?
+ What makes someone memorable?
+ What makes someone lovable?
+ What is your favorite memory? Why?
+ If you could come back as anyone from history, who would you like to be? Why?
+ What is the biggest problem facing the environment today? What can you do to help solve that problem?
+ Would you choose to stay in the country in which you live forever and never have the opportunity to travel outside of that country, or would you prefer to travel the world, but never return to the country in which you are currently living?
+ If you could create a new country, where would it be? What would the people be like? What language would be spoken? What food would the people eat? How would the economy function? Who would you elect as your leader? What would your flag look like? What would the landscape look like? Would you want to live there? Why or why not?
+ What is your favorite movie? Why?
+ What is one piece of advice you would give to all adults?
+ What is your favorite smell? Why?
+ Is there an alternative to school? If so, what would it be and how would people learn?
+ If you could change one part of our history, what would you change and why?
+ If you were to create a superhero, what would be his or her superpower? What would be the name of your superhero?
+ What is the nicest thing someone has ever done for you? Have you been able to return the favor?
+ Do you think people should have to work to earn money? If they didn't work, how would people pay for food, housing, healthcare, clothes, etc.? Create a new way of living.

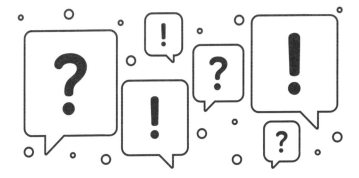

+ Would you want to work on a farm? Why or why not?
  What type of farm would you work on?
+ Do you think animals should live in captivity or in the wild?
+ What would be the perfect way to spend a winter day?
+ What would be the perfect way to spend a summer day?
+ If you had to choose only one season to live in the rest of your life,
  what would that season be?
+ Create a new ice cream flavor. What ingredients do you need for your creation?
+ Is there a secret to happiness? If so, what is it?
+ What is one thing adults do not understand?
+ Would you rather have lots of friends or a few really good friends?
+ If you didn't have school, what would you do all day?

Would you rather...

+ be old or young?
+ be a dog or a cat?
+ live in a bus or a tent?
+ learn only math or only history?
+ own a lion or an elephant?
+ always be cold or always be hot?
+ be a vegan or a carnivore?
+ have 10 siblings or none?
+ have big teeth or big ears?
+ have two different color eyes or two different size hands?
+ always walk barefoot or always with shoes on?
+ run across the country or bike across the country?
+ be a baker (think muffins and cakes) or a chef?
+ be a farmer or zookeeper?

Trail Games

1. Magnifying Glass
Bring a magnifying glass with you on the trail and play a game of, "What do you see?" With a magnifying glass, examine the following: a leaf, a rock, a flower, a crystal or other trail finds. Search for bugs, patterns, lines, and other incredible discoveries.

2. Swiss Franc Game
Find things on the trail that are roughly the size of a Swiss Franc (do not pick living things, they are happier in their natural environment). Sketch or record as many unique items as you can that are about the same size as a Swiss Franc. To expand upon this game, search for items that fit smaller or larger coins.

3. Sketch A Scene From Your Hike
Draw something that you find interesting along your route, or draw a scene of the mountain hut where you will stay overnight once you reach your destination. This can be sketched in a small notebook or a blank postcard, which can be later mailed to a friend or family member.

4. Scent Challenge
How many different things can you smell along the trail? Write them down. By playing this game, children learn to activate and rely on their senses, which is essential for situational awareness.

5. Blindfold Challenge
When you take a break on the trail, blindfold someone in the group using a bandana or a scarf and hand him or her items that are close by. By using only your sense of touch, smell and hearing, you must identify the item placed in your hand. Can you do it? The person who identifies the most items correctly wins!

6. How Many Animals
Count the number of different animals you encounter along the trail. Did you see goats, sheep, cows, chickens, dogs, marmots, etc.? Remember the number of animals you discovered while hiking and see if you can discover more on your next hike. You may catalogue the animals you discovered on the "Creature Scavenger Hunt" page in this chapter.

7. Frog Discovery

During the early spring months and during the summer, frog eggs and frogs may be abundant in the mountains. Look in wet spots, such as, under rocks, in small holes with water, on wet grass, and of course, ponds and lakes. Watch the frogs swim and hop and check which part of the life cycle they are currently in. For a detailed overview of the frog lifecycle, check page 334 of the book!

8. Constellation Game

Have your children draw a few of the most visible constellations in the Northern Hemisphere (Little Dipper, Big Dipper and Orion) in a sketch pad. During the evening and on a clear night, observe the night sky with your children.

Binntalhütte, Weissmieshütte and Maighelshütte are ideal locations to view the night sky. Step outside as darkness falls and see what constellations you can witness in the sky. To learn more about the planets and our solar system, visit the planet theme route from Weisshorn to Bella-Tola. The planetarium at St-Luc is worth the visit!

9. Animal Prints on the Trail

During the winter months, when snow is on the ground, have your hikers/snowshoers search for animal prints on the trail. Ask your children where the animal prints came from. Are they from a dog? A fox? Perhaps a deer, or another animal.

10. Place a Bet

When the going gets tough on the trail, take a moment to ask each member of the group what time they think you will reach your final destination. Record your answers in the "Notes" app on your cell phone, or on a piece of paper. Once you arrive at your destination, check to see which group member had the closest guess. What does the winner receive your group must decide, but we opt for cake; always cake!

Parenting Tip

If your child is having a particularly difficult day on the trail, assign your child a job. By providing children with a task, they feel more engaged in the activities and will be far more likely to continue the journey. We list a few ideas below.

- Provide your child with the map of your route and encourage him or her to lead the group.

- Have your child be the official flower-, special stone-, or animal-spotter by pointing out each gem along the trail.

- Encourage your child to take photos of your hike to assist in remembering the day. Help your child get creative with the camera. Remind them to look up, look down, and to capture candid shots of your family. For inspiration and support with this task, look at the "Photo Challenge" in this chapter.

Gratitude Activity

Giving thanks is a great way to pay homage to the little things in life. At the end of each day, as you gather around the dinner table, ask your group what they are most grateful for. In our family, we usually ask each member to list three things they were grateful for about the day. There are no wrong or right answers when it comes to completing this activity, and we assure you, the responses from your children may surprise you. This small, yet heartwarming exercise is the ideal way to bring your family together after a long day on the trail.

Suggestion

Document your family's responses and reflect on them in the future to ignite fond memories of your adventures.

The gratitude activity can be expanded upon by asking the following:

- What was most enjoyable about the day?

- What surprised you the most about the day?

- What made you laugh today?

- What was the most beautiful thing you saw on the trail?

Rega - Swiss Air Rescue

In 2020, two members of our Fresh Air family had the opportunity to meet with crew-members of the Rega (Swiss Air Rescue) team to learn more about their work. As you hike through the Alps, see if you can spot the Rega helicopters, which are identifiable by their red and white color, the word "Rega" inscribed somewhere on the aircraft and sometimes the numbers 1414 on the helicopter.

We list some interesting facts about the Rega helicopters for you below. This team of highly skilled individuals work very hard to answer distress calls throughout Switzerland and in the mountains. They are also responsible for transporting injured and sick patients.

- Dr. Rudolf Bucher founded Rega in April of 1952.

- The Rega phone number in Switzerland is 1414.

- There are roughly 385 employees.

- Rega is funded almost entirely by over 3 million private donors.

- Rega has 18 rescue helicopters.

- Rega is available 24 hours a day, 365 days of the year.

- Each helicopter is staffed with a pilot, a paramedic and a flight doctor.

- The helicopters need to be ready for take-off in just five minutes.

- The helicopters can fly for approximately two-hours
  at a time before they must refuel.

- Basel Rega covers a 50 km area, which can take the crew to Germany, France
  and Switzerland.

- The main reason they fly is to assist with accidents,
  and the second is to assist with transfers and medical assistance by air.

- Rega completes thousands of rescue missions each year.

- There are 13 Rega bases in Switzerland including the EMS call center in Zurich.

- The next time you see a Rega aircraft flying overhead, send up a silent
  "thank you," for all the important work they do each and every day.

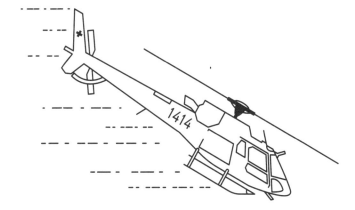

Keep Your Eyes Open – CH Rocks Original

Did you know that there is a talented group of individuals that paint and hide special rocks along trails throughout Switzerland? Well, there are, and when you find a rock you will feel a rush of excitement. When hiking through the Alps, our family has been lucky enough to discover several colorfully painted stones.

What is the point of the rocks and how do they work?

Great question! If you find a rock, you may either keep the rock, or pick it up and hide it in another spot for someone else to find, unless the rock states otherwise. You may even create your own rocks and hide them on the routes you hike for other families, individuals or hikers to find. Be careful where you place your rocks though, as you want people to be able to spot them along the route.

What do the stones look like?

All the stones are special and hand painted, typically with acrylic paint and then varnished. The rocks never contain any items that are glued on or placed onto the stones as that could potentially harm the environment or animals that come across the stones. We never want to harm the environment or nature with our creations.

The next time you are out hiking, keep your eyes open for a painted stone.

To view the type of rocks people paint and to post found rocks, conduct an internet search for "CH Rocks Original."

The Solar System

As you walk along the planet trail (in St-Luc), think about the world above you. The sun is not a planet, but rather a star that sits in the center of the solar system. This star is so hot and so intense, that you should never attempt to look at it in the sky without using the proper equipment. The sun is a vital source of energy for the Earth. At the planetarium located in St-Luc, there is a telescope that provides a safe and effective way to look at the sun. If the planetarium is open during your visit and they have the time, ask them if you can have a quick look at the sun. What you see will certainly be impressive!

The solar system consists of eight planets. Those eight planets are:

- Mercury

- Venus

- Earth (we live on Earth)

- Mars
  (some people think we might inhabit Mars in the future. What do you think?)

- Jupiter

- Saturn

- Uranus

- Neptune

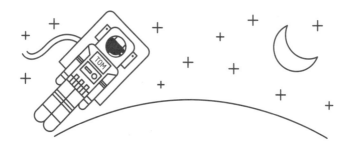

Activity

Find one fun fact about each planet as you discover them on the planet trail. Write down your fact in a notebook or on a piece of paper. Quiz your parents at the end of the day and see what they remember about the planets you came across on the trail.

Fun Facts

Twelve astronauts have been to the moon. Until now, all twelve have been American astronauts.

Pluto

Pluto was once considered a planet, but was downgraded in 2006 and is now known as a dwarf planet, along with Ceres and Eris. Poor Pluto!

Stars and Planets

Do you know how to tell the difference between a star and a planet? Well, stars tend to twinkle or shimmer in the night sky and planets do not. Planets also contain color. For example, Mars is usually red or pink in color, whereas Venus may appear light yellow in color. Planets are also typically brighter than stars.

There are several apps to assist in spotting constellations in the night sky. Have your phone with your app of choice on hand when observing the sky.

Draw a picture of the solar system.

The Life Cycle of a Frog

Frogs are incredible creatures and often seen in abundance in the mountains. The life cycle of a frog is pretty interesting and starts when a mature frog lays eggs. Those eggs then grow into a tadpole, which then forms two, then four legs, before making its transition into a froglet. The life cycle of a frog is complete when the froglet finally grows into an adult frog. When you observe frogs in nature, ask yourself: What phase of life is this frog currently in? Is it a tadpole with two legs, a froglet or an adult frog?

Metamorphosis

Metamorphosis is a big word with lots of syllables, but what does that word actually mean? Fantastic question! Metamorphosis is a biological (think living things) term that means to change form or shape. There are several creatures in the natural world that go through metamorphosis. Now it is your job to name a few.

Below you will find a sketch of the frog life cycle. If you would like, color in the picture and don't forget to look for frog eggs or frogs on your next adventure! Oh, and be careful when hiking on the trails because if you look closely, you might just discover tiny frogs along the path.

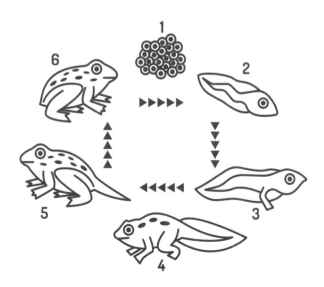

1. Eggs

2. Tadpole

3. Tadpole with 2 legs

4. Tadpole with 4 legs

5. Froglet

6. Adult frog

The Creature Scavenger Hunt

Listed below are creatures both big and small that we have personally seen while hiking in Switzerland. Can you spot these animals while you are hiking?

If you are not sure where to look, remember a few important clues.

● Salamanders and frogs love wet, damp places. Be careful when hiking during the rain or after a rainstorm, as these critters may cross your path.

● Alpine newts and fish can be seen in Alpine lakes.

● Ibex and chamois are typically seen at higher elevations and enjoy climbing on rocky terrain.

● Zermatt is known for its Black Nose sheep and we loved spending time with them when we stayed at Hotel Schwarzsee.

● Marmots are often heard before they are seen. These animals make an almost bird like or whistle sound. Look for them coming out of holes in the ground or perched on rocks.

● Foxes are typically nocturnal creatures, meaning they come out at night. Look for their glowing eyes in the evening hours if you are looking for stars.

● Hawks are often seen flying overhead and make a lovely sound.

● Cows are virtually everywhere; just listen for the bells.

Remember, it might take you several hikes, or even a year or more to witness all the creatures below. Be patient; keep your eyes open and your binoculars ready.

Creature	Date	Location
Salamander		
Alpine Newt		
Ladybug		
Frog Eggs		
Tadpoles		
Frog		
Marmot		
Ibex		
Chamois		
Caterpillar		
Fish		
Hawk		
Goat		
Butterfly		
Fox		
Red Deer		
Squirrel		
Black Nose Sheep		
Cow		
Bearded Eagle		

The Color Scavenger Hunt

Excluding any item on yourself including clothes, your backpack, shoes and colors on those people around you, your job is to find all of the colors listed below on the trail. Once you discover the color, you may write down your discovery using words or pictures. You may complete this activity as a group or as individuals.

Hint: Variations of the colors count too, for example, light blue, dark green, etc.

Did you know the blue in nature is actually a very rare color? Well, it is. If you don't believe us, look it up and see what you learn.

Color	Word or Picture
Red:	
Orange:	
Yellow:	
Green:	
Blue:	

Purple:

Pink:

White:

Black:

Gray:

Turquoise:

(your choice):

(your choice):

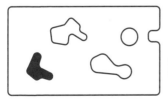

Flower Finder

Pictured below you will find some of the most common flowers in the Swiss Alps, as well as a few elusive ones. See how many flowers you can find while you are on the trail, but please remember not to pick the flowers. You can track where you saw a specific flower below. Keep in mind, some of these may come in several varieties. Have fun spotting these colorful treasures throughout your journeys!

Tip: Keep your eyes open for the Lady Slipper, which is a type of orchid. They are rare and not often seen on the trails.

1. Spring Crocus
Frühlings-Krokus / Crocus de printemps

Date of Discovery:

Color of Flower:

---

2. Primrose
Stängellose Schlüsselblume / Primevère commune

Date of Discovery:

Color of Flower:

---

3. Forget-Me-Not
Wald-Vergissmeinnicht / Myosotis des bois

Date of Discovery:

Color of Flower:

4. Spring Gentian
Frühlings–Enzian / Gentiane printanière

Date of Discovery:

Color of Flower:

---

5. Narrow Leaf Cottongrass
Schmalblättriges Wollgras / Linaigrette à feuilles étroites

Date of Discovery:

Color of Flower:

---

6. Scheuchzer's Bellflower
Scheuchzers Glockenblume / Campanule de Scheuchzer

Date of Discovery:

Color of Flower:

---

7. Alpine Rose
Rostblättrige Alpenrose / Rhododendron ferrugineux

Date of Discovery:

Color of Flower:

8. Common Bird's-Foot Trefoil
Gewöhnlicher Hornklee / Lotier corniculé

Date of Discovery:

Color of Flower:

---

9. Red Campion
Rote Waldnelke / Compagnon rouge

Date of Discovery:

Color of Flower:

---

10. Mountain Buttercup
Berg-Hahnenfuss / Renoncule des montagnes

Date of Discovery:

Color of Flower:

---

11. Globeflower
Europäische Trollblume / Trolle d'Europe

Date of Discovery:

Color of Flower:

12. Field Scabious
Feld-Witwenblume / Knautie des champs

Date of Discovery:

Color of Flower:

---

13. Lady Slipper
Frauenschuh / Sabot de Vénus

Date of Discovery:

Color of Flower:

---

14. Dark Mullein
Dunkles Wollkraut / Molène noire

Date of Discovery:

Color of Flower:

---

15. Cobweb Houseleek
Spinnweb-Hauswurz / Joubarbe aranéeuse

Date of Discovery:

Color of Flower:

16. Common Spotted Orchid
Gefleckte Fingerwurz / Orchis tacheté

Date of Discovery:

Color of Flower:

---

17. Bladder Campion
Gemeines Leimkraut / Silène enflé

Date of Discovery:

Color of Flower:

---

18. French Willow
Wald-Weidenröschen / Epilobe à feuilles étroites

Date of Discovery:

Color of Flower:

Photo Challenges

Parents: Please note, that any type of camera may be used during these challenges. This challenge works wonders for turning tough days on the trail into successful excursions. Trust us!

By encouraging children to take part in a photo challenge, they are learning a host of useful skills. As the adult, please take the time to teach your child the following when it comes to the photo challenge.

+ Focus (near, far, macro, etc.)
+ Zoom (lens and digital)
+ Capturing movement
  (speed of the object, movement of the photographer, speed of the camera)
+ How to use the flash and when the flash is necessary.
  Experiment by placing different colored paper in front of the flash.

Proper Handling/Use of the Camera

+ Take precautions with cameras in wet weather.
+ Try to avoid touching the lens and keep the lens clean.
+ Never place a camera face down on the lens
  and always place the lens cover on the lens for protection.
+ Be careful with cameras in extreme temperatures.

Photo Challenge Number 1

To get started with the photo challenge, consider one of the following themes to initiate the activity. Your child will be asked to capture one or more of the following while on the trail:

+ Something wet
+ Something cold
+ Something hot
+ Something with stripes or dots
+ A specific color (pick a color other than green, brown, gray or yellow)
+ Capture the current season
+ Capture something in bloom
+ Something with letters

Once your child has completed the task, either create his or her own folder on the computer with their work, or print their favorite photo for a nature journal.

Photo Challenge Number 2

Can your child capture three of the objects below with his or her camera?

+ An insect on a flower or a leaf
+ A bird in flight
+ People – take photos of friends or family members on the trail
+ Flowers in a field
+ A butterfly
+ A tree either coming into bloom or during the autumn season
+ Delicious – capture a meal during your hiking adventure
+ Something out-of-place – whenever you spot something that just doesn't belong, snap a photo of the out-of-place object
+ Unique – take a photo of something that is extra special along the trail
+ Fun – take a fun or a funny image on the trail

Photo Challenge Number 3

The Macro Photo Challenge

Have your child identify something in nature, such as a bug, a flower, a leaf, a fruit, a stone, etc. Once your child has located the object he or she wishes to capture, have your child zoom in on that object until only a small portion of the object comes into focus. Have your child take the photo and share it with the group. The group must now identify what the object is in its entirety. You will need a steady hand to capture a clear image!

Other Photo Challenge Ideas:

- Shoot reflections of people, objects, etc. in bodies of water. These create some of our favorite pictures.

- Be creative when shooting, don't just take a picture, but create an image or a piece of art.

- Look at tiny, little details – raindrops, insects, mushrooms, frog eggs, etc.

- Photograph just part of an object – instead of taking a photo of the entire object, just take a picture of part of the object.

- Experiment by changing the position of the object you are photographing to see how the photo changes. Which position do you prefer?

- As an emerging photographer, give your child a camera to capture a hike for the entire day. It is his or her job, as a photo journalist, to curate the day from start to finish. It will be fascinating to observe your child's perspective.

What Type of Cow is That?

No doubt you will encounter lots of cows as you hike through the Swiss Alps. There are several different breeds of cows grazing on the alpine pastures. See if you are able to determine the different breeds based on the descriptions below.

Hérens

These black, dark brown, sometimes even reddish beauties look fierce and intimating. They are stocky and strong and come from the Val d'Hérens, in the Valais region of Switzerland. These cows may be used for cow fighting, as the females tend to be quite aggressive. We saw a heard of these cows on our way down from Cabane des Violettes and felt the need to be very cautious as we walked through the herd.

Holstein

Though not native to Switzerland, these dairy cows are common throughout the country. Similar to the Fleckvieh, these are typically black and white, but they are sometimes reddish-brown and white in color. **Did you know?** Each autumn the cows are brought down from the Alps to graze on lower pastures. This is a celebrated event referred to as *Alpabfahrt*. If you have the opportunity to witness this old tradition, we highly recommend it.

Tips

Remember to have respect when walking through cow pastures. It is the job of the mother cow to protect her calf, so if you see calves in the area, walk with extreme caution.

If you are interested in learning more about cows, don't forget to visit the "Lieselotte" theme trail on your way down from Männlichen.

Simmental or Swiss Fleckvieh

These cows are light brown, or reddish and white in color, and are from the Bernese Oberland area. This cow looks a lot like the Évolène breed, but they are different. Here is a tip for differentiating the two; the Simmental cows tend to be larger in size and may contain larger patches of white on their hides than the Évolène cows. Can you spot the difference?

The Highland Cattle

This breed of cattle is one of our favorites because when they are young they look like teddy bears. These cattle are fuzzy and typically brown, with hair falling into their eyes. The breed is not native to Switzerland, but can, at times, be seen grazing in the Alps. Keep your eyes out for this furry animal!

Braunvieh

These cows are gray-brown in color with a black nose, circled with a white muzzle and fuzzy ears. Please don't tell the other cows, but we think these cows are one of the cutest breeds of cows out there. Shh...

Évolène

These cows can be identified by their color, which is either a reddish-brown, with a bit of white; or black, with a bit of white. They are from the Valais area of Switzerland.

Detective Challenge: We have provided you with images of all the cows that you may come across in Switzerland except for the Évolène breed. It is your job, based off of the description, to locate these cows while you hike through Switzerland. Were you successful?

Winter Games to Play

- Build a mini-igloo.

- Build a snowman and don't forget to give him eyes, a nose, something on top of his head and an item of your choice to place in his hands.

- Make a snow angel by lying in the snow and spreading your arms and legs out. Once you stand up, your angel will appear.

- Write your name or a happy message in the snow for the next hiker to discover.

- Word scramble – have someone in your group mix-up a common word and have the group figure out what the word spells in the snow.

- Footprint discovery – play a game of hide and go seek in the snow. This version is slightly easier than the original because the footprints of the individual hiding are quite visible in the snow.

- Frozen bubbles – if the temperature is cold enough, try blowing bubbles with bubble liquid and see if your bubbles freeze.

Tip

Another fun activity that you must try is snowshoeing. Though not necessarily easy, this is a great way to hike through the snow. Don't forget your poles!

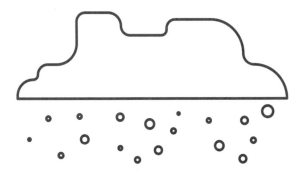

Rougemont sur les hauts 2h 50min
Saanen ✿ 4h 20min
Les Granges ✿ 30min
La Videmanette 4h 20min
La Pierreuse 3h
Col de Base 3h
Rocher du Midi 3h 40min
Plan de la Douve 3h 25min
Les Marrindes Montreux 4h 30min
Ciernes Picat 2h 10min
Pra Jean 5h 35min
La Laitemaire 2h 15min

Bettens 30min
La Vausseresse 1h 10min
Pâquier Gétaz 1h 30min
Paray Dorenaz 2h 40min

Château-d'Oex Centre 5min
Pont Turrian 20min
Cascade du Ramaclé 45min
La Montagnette 2h 25min

Château-d'Oex
Gare
986 m

78   46

Tourisme pédestre
Wanderwege

Trail Banana Bread

Banana bread is the perfect trail food. Rich with bananas, nuts, and cinnamon, this bread makes the ideal trail snack.

Encourage your children to help make this delicious bread with you. We recommend making the bread the night before, allowing it to sit overnight permitting the flavors to really soak in. Pack for long train rides and/or as a trail snack.

Ingredients

+ **3–4** ripe bananas
+ **2 tbsp** cinnamon
+ **½ tsp** vanilla
+ **1 tsp** salt
+ **1 tsp** baking soda
+ **2 cups / 230 g** flour – use flour of choice
+ **½ cup / 115 g** maple syrup
+ **1** large egg
+ **½ stick / 100 g** of butter, melted (or substitute coconut oil for butter)
+ **1 ½ cups / 130 g** of chopped walnuts or your favorite nut

Optional

For additional nutrients consider the following: Grate one carrot and/or one zucchini into the mixture. If you add these ingredients, your bread will be very moist. Add ¼ cup / 25 g chia seeds or hemp seeds.

Mash the bananas until they are soft and mushy, reserving one banana to be cut into chunks and added in. Mix bananas, maple syrup, egg and melted butter together.

Add all of the dry ingredients to the mixture. Once thoroughly mixed, add to a bread loaf pan and bake at 180°C for approximately 30–45 minutes. Baking times may vary, please check on the bread and remove when a knife/wooden stick comes out relatively clean and the top of the loaf is golden brown.

Special note, this bread can be made multiple ways. We love cinnamon, so we typically add extra. Depending on the ripeness of our bananas we either add additional maple syrup or less. Extra nuts can be added for protein and texture. You can also make the bread loaf into muffins, but remember to decrease the baking time!

Our Hikes to Huts Adventures

Favorite Meal at a Hut

Noah: The soup and the cheese Spätzli at Berggasthaus Glattalp.
Tessa: The salad at Berggasthaus Piz Calmot on the way up to Maighelshütte SAC and the Fondue at Cabane des Violettes CAS.
Dad: Tartiflette at Auberge-Refuge La Vouivre.
Mom: Älplermagronen at Berggasthaus Meglisalp.

Favorite View(s)

Noah: The ridgeline hike from Klingenstock to Fronalpstock.
Tessa: Gemmi Lodge 2350.
Dad: The pass Widderalpsattel on the Appenzell Tour.
Mom: Leglerhütte SAC and the hike from Allmendhubel to Gimmelwald ... bliss! Shoot, one more please, the views on the Eiger Tour. Switzerland is just gorgeous!

Best Social Media Post

Noah: When my head looked stuck in a rock on the way to Binntalhütte SAC.
Tessa: Chateau d'Oex Hot Air Balloon Festival.
Dad: Eiger north face on route to Berghaus Alpiglen.
Mom: Arriving at the tiny village in Meglisalp. Wow! Noah holding a chicken on the way to Bollenwees and Tessa talking to the goats on that same route.

Best Hut to Witness a Sunrise

Noah: Gemmi Lodge 2350
Tessa: Auberge du Grand-Sommartel
Dad: Auberge de Salanfe when the sun illuminated the peaks in an orange glow above the lake.
Mom: Fronalpstock, Stoss – hike up in the dark and watch the magic unfold! Epic!

Favorite Animal(s) Discovered on the Trail

Noah: Kittens at the Farm Bucheli, Black Nose sheep in Zermatt, and the gigantic moth near Refuge Giacomini
Tessa: Big moth, baby frogs, salamanders, chamois
Dad: Black Nose sheep in Zermatt
Mom: The herd of chamois in Zermatt

Favorite Lake

Noah: Auberge-Refuge La Vouivre
Tessa: The pond at Leglerhütte SAC
Dad: Theodulgletschersee, it's like a moonscape, and if you look closely, you will discover garnets (red crystals) in the rocks.
Mom: I have to cheat on this one. I love the four lakes, one pass hike from Melchsee-Frutt to Trübsee. All of the lakes along that route are amazing!

Best Winter Excursion

Noah: Auberge du Grand-Sommartel
Tessa: Chateau d'Oex Hot Air Balloon Festival
Dad: Chalet du Soldat
Mom: Chalet du Soldat

Best Alpine Playground

Noah: Berghaus Männlichen and the Kid's Paradise in Elm
Tessa: Berghaus Männlichen
Dad: Sörenberg
Mom: Allmendhubel

Best Theme Trail

Noah: Elm Giant Forest
Tessa: Lieselotte at Männlichen
Dad: All the trails, nature is the best teacher!
Mom: Matterhorn Glacier Trail, but know that this trail might just break your heart as the future of glaciers looks pretty bleak.

Best Educational Route/Location

Noah: The Planets Trail, starting from Hotel Weisshorn
Tessa: St-Luc Observatory – looking at the sun through a telescope was interesting
Dad: Want to know more about...
+ dams = Salanfe,
+ or bells = Selamatt,
+ or geology = Binntal,
+ or glaciers = Zermatt,
+ or watchmaking = Le Locle,
+ or planets = St-Luc.
Mom: St. Martin, the history of that little hamlet is fascinating.

Favorite Memory

Noah: Finding snakes at Lac de Taney and discovering the three kittens at the Bucheli Farm.

Tessa: Petting the Black Nose sheep because they are so cute!

Dad: The tiny grass frogs at Golzersee, so small! Also, when we were in Zermatt and Melinda was corralled by the Black Nose sheep, that was funny!

Mom: Seriously, just one, it simply isn't possible. I loved watching my children eat fondue for the first time at Cabane des Violettes CAS on the Swiss National Day. I cherished the moments of our family playing with the friendly Black Nose sheep in Zermatt. I adored the views from the Fronalpstock ridgeline hike and completing that one with my son as we ran to the finish. I treasured listening to the alphorns and yodelers at Windgällenhütte. Watching hail pound the terrain in August at Cabane des Violettes CAS was pretty epic. Oh, and did I mention listening to the six alphorns playing at Berghotel Seebenalp? Amazing!

Counts

- **Kilometers Hiked (2019 & 2020):** 351 in 2019 & approximately 340 in 2020

- **Hours of Hiking (2019 & 2020):** 222 h

- **Ascent (2019 & 2020):** 22,850 m

- **Descent (2019 & 2020):** 31,550 m

- **Salamanders:** 27

- **Marmot Spottings:** 12

- **Chamois:** 21

- **Ibex:** 6

- **Blisters:** 13

- **Lakes:** 33

- **Ice Creams:** 33

- **Cakes:** 49 (apple, apricot, blueberry and plum, though our favorite is always apple with whipped cream! It just doesn't get any better.)

Epilogue

And there you have it; our love story for natural spaces has come to an end. A devotion to a country that feels like a gift that we continue to have the privilege of opening. Will we be back? The truth is, we hope to never leave. Our hearts have been touched by the beauty of flowering meadows, jagged peaks, and turquoise lakes. We intend to keep exploring and learning for the rest of our lives. Plus, we must continue to fulfill what we believe to be one of our greatest responsibilities as parents: To venture far and wide with our children so that they too come to realize that nature is not just a pastime, but a necessity.

The natural world calls to us and invites us to explore with intention. A world that needs our help. And with that, we feel compelled to continue. To walk amongst mountains and shooting stars. To appreciate the wonderous and the miraculous. For us, there is no other place we would rather be.

Fresh Air Kids Switzerland
52 Inspiring Hikes That Will Make Kids and Parents Happy

Discover Switzerland with the kids

This wittily designed hiking guide is the perfect companion for families who would like to spend more time outdoors and discover the multifaceted hiking country that is Switzerland. In a simple and playful way, the necessary basic knowledge for family-friendly hiking is imparted and a host of activities are offered to make children and parents happy. With these 52 well-thought-out hikes, all you have to do is put on your hiking boots and get started!

+ 52 easy-to-difficult hikes and outdoor adventures
   for the whole family
+ Inspiring photos
+ Practical information for each hike

Authors: Melinda & Robert Schoutens
Illustrator: Felix Kindelán
Pages: 272
ISBN: 978-2-940481-62-0

Fresh Air Kids Switzerland
My Book of Discoveries

Hello Fresh Air Kids!

This book of discoveries was created just for you. It includes an exciting bouquet of activities, such as a scavenger hunt, a summer bucket list, coloring pages and your own personal hiking ABC. You will also find lots of pages to track your hikes. Fill them out and draw or glue in things you collect along the way. You will always remember what you record.

+ The perfect companion for the bestseller *Fresh Air Kids Switzerland*
+ Entertaining activities and illustrations for children from 6 years old and above
+ Track hikes and create memories
+ In 3 languages (E/D/F) for additional and playful learning
+ Small and handy: fits in any backpack
  and ideal for long train rides

Authors: Melinda & Robert Schoutens
Illustrator: Felix Kindelán
Pages: 64
ISBN: 978-2-940481-65-1

Fresh Air Kids Switzerland
Hikes to Huts: Adventures for the Kid Inside Us All

ISBN: 978-3-907293-23-2
First Edition 2021

Text and photos: Melinda and Robert Schoutens
Cover and layout design: Felix Kindelán, Vanessa Larson
Proofreading: Karin Waldhauser

First edition, May 2021
Deposit of a mandatory copy in Switzerland: May 2021

Printed in the Czech Republic

© 2021 Helvetiq (RedCut Sàrl),
Côtes de Montbenon 30, CH-1003 Lausanne
All rights reserved

HELVETIQ benefits from structural support
from the Federal Office of Culture for the years 2021-2024.

www.helvetiq.com